The Fear Factor

The Fear Factor

Terry Prone

LONDUBH BOOKS

First published in 2011 by
Londubh Books
18 Casimir Avenue, Harold's Cross, Dublin 6w, Ireland
www.londubh.ie
1 3 5 4 2
Origination by Londubh Books; cover by redrattledesign
Printed by Scandbooks, Smedjebacken, Sweden
ISBN: 978-1-907535-23-9

Acknowledgements

Countless clients of the Communications Clinic shared their fears with me on condition that I didn't identify them. They know who they are and I thank them. Colleagues, particularly Tom Savage, Stephanie Brady, Barry McLaughlin, Aileen Gaskin, Pauline Ní Luanaigh and Eoghan McDermott contributed greatly. Thanks also to Dr Edmond Smyth and Professor Hilary Humphreys for their expertise on bugs. Oops. Bacteria.

Portions of this book appeared in another form in the *Irish Examiner*, the *Evening Herald*, *Image* and *Woman's Way*.

For my boss, Anton Savage

Contents

Introduction

I figure I meet more frightened people in any given week than does the average psychiatrist.

I meet people who are frightened of media, either because they know a newspaper is doing a story about them and the likelihood is that it's going to be negative, or because they have to go on radio or TV and believe their chances of coming out of the studio alive and with their reputation intact are small.

I meet people who have to make a speech at their daughter's wedding, or a presentation to the President of their multinational corporation, and who haven't slept since they were told about this challenge.

I meet people who have to go in front of an examination board who will decide if they know enough about healthcare to move closer to becoming a doctor, or don't.

I meet people who are terrified of losing their job or their seat in the Dáil.

I meet people who are going into court and are in awe of it, or who have to announce redundancies and are eaten alive with fear of the task.

I meet people who have to tell those closest to them a secret, new or old, to which their loved ones are not, currently, privy, whether that's the fact that they had a baby before they married and that the child is now grown up and eager to meet their half-siblings, or that they've received a diagnosis of terminal illness.

I meet people who are afraid of being discriminated against, people afraid of flying, people afraid of driving.

I even meet people who are afraid of me. That one always catches me unawares. Particularly since the Botox. (See page 161.)

Most of the time, people want me to take their fear away.

Now, I'll do a lot for money, but take your fear away? No. Not possible. I can, however, help *you* to take your fear way. Or, in most cases, use your fear as fuel, allowing you to do what you want to do.

'I want you to make me less nervous,' a client will say, when they're outlining what they want to achieve.

It's the wrong place to start, when you're looking at public performance. You *should* be fearful, if you're an actor or a public speaker, before you walk out on to the stage. Look at it this way. If you're an actor, you have to take an audience made up of perhaps six hundred total strangers, make them pay attention to you, make them believe – for two or three hours – that you are a Prince of Denmark or the Prince's girlfriend or an ageing American salesman. You have to make them laugh, make them cry and send them out of the theatre seeing the world in a subtly or deeply different way. Of course you should be fearful.

Similarly, if you want to do a speech which will make people look at you, your business, the nation or a particular issue anew, it is appropriate for you to be fearful, because if you fail, this failure will have serious consequences.

So you shouldn't reject the fear but you must be able to manage it. And it's the same, whether you're scared of wasps, death, ghosts, planes or your boss. One of the most dangerous things that could happen is for you to lose your capacity to be frightened – which occasionally happens and does the person involved no good at all.

This book is not DIY therapy for terror, although it will cover some of the methods to manage fear, whether in the context of an upcoming media performance or a speech at your daughter's wedding, or in the context of paralysing fear of flying.

It's an examination of the things that terrify us and the things that terrified our grandparents. Sometimes they're the same. Sometimes they're very different. It's a look at the things that may frighten you and the things you think other people are idiotic to be frightened about: flying, bugs, water, heights, death, holidays.

One of the realities of this topic is that laughter is a great enemy of fear. So, with luck, you'll find aspects of *The Fear Factor* that will make you laugh.

If you discover that I've missed your pet fear, forgive me and contact us at Londubh, where the website (www.londubh.ie) awaits your special terror.

So – as the pilots say while you curl your toes in panic before take-off – sit back, make yourself comfortable and enjoy the flight. Or, to put it more bluntly, brace yourself…

1

Fear Itself and Why It Matters

You can't do without fear. You may think a life without fear would be a happier life but it would, in fact, be a much more dangerous way to live.

One part of our brain – the amygdala – has a starring role in terror. The amygdala is made up of two almond-shaped portions of the mid-section of the brain, near the ears, so named from the Greek work for an almond, and it seems to be a phenomenal processor of threatening data. It's the portion of our mind that says, '*Waaa*, big black bear.'

'It is the brain which sees, not the eye,' says historian James Burke. 'Reality is in the brain before it is experienced, or else the signals we get from the eye would make no sense.'

In rats, it takes twelve one-thousands of a second for the '*Waaa*' message to get to the amygdala through what's called the thalmic pathway. One neuroscientist has dubbed this the 'low road,' as opposed to the 'high road' which is the route taken by incoming information to the parts of the brain where analytical functioning takes place.

At its crudest, it could be portrayed like this. The low road means you register a big black presence and your entire body reacts: stress hormones pump into your system, your sweat takes on a particular smell and you freeze: *Waaa*. All within a fraction of a second. Like the rats. The high road means you realise either 'Oh, this is a model of a black bear – it's not real, I can relax,' or, 'This bear is the real thing and I'd better get my skates on.' The low road means your body is ready to run like hell. The high road means that you clutch your own throat and laugh at having mistaken a moth-eaten stuffed bear for the real thing, the adrenalin disperses and the shakes disappear.

'The mind operates most efficiently by relegating a good deal of high-level, sophisticated thinking to the unconscious, just as a modern jetliner is able to fly on automatic pilot with little or no input from the human, "conscious" pilot', says Timothy D. Wilson, Professor of Psychology at the University of Virginia. 'The adaptive unconscious does an excellent job of sizing up the world, warning people of danger, setting goals, and initiating action in a sophisticated and efficient manner.'

The amygdala and related structures add up to that 'sophisticated and efficient' capacity to make split-second decisions to fight or flee. Interest in the amygdala is relatively recent, sparked a few decades ago when it was discovered that destroying the region of a monkey's brain that included the amygdala had an astonishing end result.

'The monkeys no longer seemed to understand the emotional significance of objects in their environment, even though they had no trouble recognising, identifying or remembering them,' wrote Drew Westen, who's a professor in the departments of Psychiatry and Psychology at Emory University in Atlanta, Georgia. 'They would eat faeces or other inedible objects that normally elicited disgust or indifference, and they were no longer afraid of things that had previously led to fear. With "reason" intact but emotion incapacitated, these monkey were generally unable to use their emotions to guide their behaviour.'

But it's not just monkeys that suffer when bits of their frontal cortex, related to the amygdala, are damaged. Damage to that area of the human brain makes the individual 'blind to the future'. They see no consequences to their actions and they see no danger in their surroundings, which, if you think about it, makes their surroundings incredibly dangerous. In a riot, someone with an intact brain looks at a mounted police officer and thinks, 'That's a ton of horseflesh. I don't want it to sidle into me or bite me or stamp on me.' Someone with damage to the areas of their brain governing fear makes no such sensible deductions.

It's a little like that other rare condition, where the individual never feels pain. Pain is a red light that says, 'Danger.' If you don't feel pain, you can be beaten, burned or cut and – while you may be fascinated by what's happening to your body – you don't feel it, so you never think to protect yourself. Similarly, if you can't feel fear, you won't concentrate on what you need to concentrate on in a dangerous situation.

Fear, then, is a good emotion.

It may not feel good, but it undoubtedly ensured the survival of the human species. It also created some of the world's great art. The cave paintings in France and Spain show massive, terrifying animals, and where humans appear, they are tiny and drawn in much less detail: testament to just how fragile the hunters of more than thirty thousand years ago knew themselves to be, compared to the scale of the beasts they needed to kill if they were to eat.

The cave paintings are filled with worshipful admiration of the big beasts on which the hunters depended – but they may also have been a method of reducing fear: 'See, even though we are minuscule, compared to the vastness of what we hunt, we nonetheless bring it down by our collective efforts.'

Much later, in the Middle Ages, when the Black Death struck, people took to the hills, literally, to get away from the disease which had been delivered to port cities by arriving ships. They had no idea how the illness was transmitted, but fear led them away from the crowded conditions which were killing vast tranches of the population of the time. It also led to the creation of one of the great books – still in print – Bocaccio's *Decameron*, an account of those fear-driven city exiles and the raunchy, riotously funny stories they tell each other to keep themselves entertained in their chosen exile.

Down the centuries, fear has led to war and to streams of refugees moving back and forth across the continent of Europe. At an individual level, fear has led to the creation of ghost stories and the development of magical potions to ward off spirits and visits from the devil. Each century and each era presents humanity with a different set of potential fears – and reminds us of just how important the emotion is to our survival.

In our own time, Gavin de Becker, a man who makes his living by advising the rich and famous on how to avoid being raped, brutalised or kidnapped, maintains that fear is a gift we should cherish. He's even written a book with that title – *The Gift of Fear* – a central theme of which is that the best asset in the prevention of violence to oneself lies in intuition.

'It may be hard to accept its importance,' he admits, 'because intuition is usually looked upon by us thoughtful Western beings with contempt. It is often described as emotional, unreasonable, or inexplicable. Husbands chide their wives about "feminine intuition" and don't take it seriously. If intuition is used by a woman to explain some choice she made or a concern she can't let go of, men roll their eyes and write it off. We much prefer logic, the grounded, explainable, unemotional thought process that ends in a supportable conclusion.'

De Becker's experience in working with victims of apparently random violence, is that intuition, or 'gut feeling,' as men prefer to call it, can be a powerful warning sign that should not be ignored. If, instinctively, being in a situation or close to an individual makes you fearful, don't dismiss your own sense of unease. Examine the evidence you have subconsciously amassed and take the right action. Do not, in short, make like Julius Caesar.

The fifteenth of March was a day when, if he had responded to intuition, Caesar would have rolled over in the bed, slept in and done nothing more than a little pottering in the garden of his villa. For starters, a fortune teller had already announced that the Ides of March would write *finis* to Caesar's life and reign. This fortune teller didn't operate like American meteorologists, who are a cross between Paddy Power and John Eagleton, mixing gambling with meteorology: 'Tomorrow will bring a 60 per cent chance of rain.' No, this fortune teller simply said the Ides of March would be fatal to Caesar. Perhaps because she knew of this grim prediction, Caesar's wife, Calpurnia, begged him not to leave the house on the fifteenth, as she had dreamed of his death the night before. Caesar was about to cave in and stay home for the day when his old friend Decimus Brutus arrived and slagged him off for listening to such nonsense. Caesar pulled himself together and left for Pompey's Theatre. The rational information he received from Brutus caused him to disregard the intuition he had been about to acknowledge and act upon.

On the way, a passerby stopped Caesar and begged him to read a petition. The parchment warned Caesar that plotters were planning to assassinate him. Useful intelligence, which, had Caesar bothered to read it, could have saved his life. But he shoved the parchment in the back pocket of his toga, or wherever he stored random incoming documents, and continued on his way. Within minutes, Brutus and several others had stabbed him to death.

It's eminently possible that during his journey to his death, Caesar may have made a joke about the danger he was in. That's one of the ways in which intuition manifests itself. The endangered person receives evidence that they are under some kind of threat. They do not take the threat seriously enough to take action to avoid it, but – below the level of awareness – they are sufficiently rattled to make a joke. The joke seems to be a way of comforting oneself in the face of danger.

A classic example was provided by one of the lethal episodes in the brief, mad, murderous career of Theodore Kaczynski, an academic who withdrew from work and contact with people in the late 1970s, living a hermit-like existence in an isolated Montana cabin. Starting in 1978, Kaczynski made sporadic visits to his local post office, to send off home-made pipe bombs to educational establishments and businesses. The recipients, three of whom died, twenty-three of whom were injured, had no idea who had sent them a killing gift.

The unseen and unknown killer was called the 'Unabomber', until he issued a rambling diatribe which was carried in *The New York Times*. At that point, Kaczynski's brother recognised some of the phraseology in the 'manifesto' as typical of his reclusive brother and told the FBI. As a result Theodore is now serving several life sentences without possibility of parole.

One of the heavy pipe-bomb packages mailed by the Unabomber went to the California Forestry Association, addressed to a man who no longer worked there. A few management executives discussed what to do about it. They didn't check the address from which it was supposed to have come. If they had, they'd have found it was fictitious. Instead, they decided to open it. While not overtly disagreeing with that decision, one of the men present must have had inchoate doubts about it because he stood up and cracked a joke.

'I'm going back to my office before the bomb goes off,' he said.

Before he reached his own desk, the bomb *had* gone off, killing the colleague who opened it.

'Humour, particularly dark humour, is a common way to communicate true concern without the risk of feeling silly afterwards, and without overtly showing fear,' Gavin de Becker writes. 'The point is, though, that the idea came into consciousness. Why? Because all the information was there. The package sent by the Unabomber to the California Forestry Association was very heavy. It was covered with tape, had too much postage, and aroused enough interest that morning that several people speculated on whether it might be a bomb.'

What each of the group mentally dismissed as a rejectable 'gut feeling' was in fact an evidenced, real fear that could have saved a life. The key point here is that we're smarter than we realise at spotting danger and protecting ourselves from it – except when we decide that our fear is silly and that we should ignore it, or when we have no framework into which to fit our fear. We'd never do anything if we paid attention to all the fears that are illogical, irrational and based on no evidence whatever. On the other hand, when things don't add up, the arithmetic should sometimes be examined more rigorously. If a group of young foreigners want to learn how to fly a plane but have weirdly little interest in takeoffs and landings, that could be dismissed as simply peculiar. In fact, it was dismissed as no more than strange or weird. But, as we learned the day the planes rammed into the Twin Towers, it wasn't weird at all. The men involved were never going to take off at the controls of a passenger jet, so the mechanics of take-off were unimportant to them. Nor were they ever planning to land a plane. It was the bit in the middle – and *only* the bit in the middle – about which they needed to know.

Several people in several different US agencies who encountered Mohammed Atta and his colleagues before they ploughed planes into buildings were uneasy about them, but had no framework into which to fit their unease. The unease was because the terrorists leaked the truth about themselves constantly.

This always happens. Human beings are like colanders. Fill them up with information about which they're worried or feel guilty, and they start to leak streams of truth, whether or not they want to. They behave strangely, although the strangeness may not be acknowledged by others until after the event, which can be anything from a spree shooting to a shouting match.

The attacks on the Twin Towers changed the way we live and travel. They turned every passenger into a potential terrorist. It's difficult however, to find evidence that it greatly increased the fear some people have about flying – that seems to stay at roughly the same level all the time.

As will become clear later in the book, those with severe phobia about flying cannot be dissuaded from their terror by rational argument. It's too deep-seated for that. It's not the only fear out of which a sufferer cannot be argued. Some fears – like arachnophobia, the fear of spiders – are objectively silly and should be ignored but some highly intelligent people cannot ignore them, because their fears have turned into disabling phobias, and even if you smack a phobia with an encyclopaedia of contrary information, together with every logical argument going, it will come out of hiding when you least expect it and smite you.

Fear of Being Stalked

Famous people attract one kind of stalker. Unknowns attract a different kind of stalker. Both are dangerous. If you have a realistic fear that you're being stalked, talk to the Gardaí immediately. They have a special unit that deals with stalking and the officers in that unit are super at their job.

Madonna has experienced celebrity stalking, as has David Letterman, the American TV presenter. Many of those stalkers are delusional, and believe that they have a relationship with the famous person.

The majority of stalking cases in Ireland are former partners or jilted lovers who won't take no for an answer. They are often emotionally abusive control freaks who dominated their partner in the relationship and viewed them as a possession. The big mistake is to try to let them down gently. They should be told that what they're doing is stalking and that you're going to report them to the Gardaí. Threats should be taken seriously.

All your friends should be warned against giving them your email address, real address or telephone number. If one of them gives the number, change your phone, conceal the number when you ring even your closest friends, and share the number only with people as dedicated to protecting you as you are. Get off Facebook.

The distinction between a fear of, say, bats, about which most people know very little and have never encountered in person, and a phobia about bats is relatively easy to establish.

Let's say you're afraid of bats. You believe them to be bloodsucking filthy flying rodents who bite, pass on disease, like to get into people's hair, have never done humanity any good and are gratuitously protected by the EU.

Now consider the following. Bats are really cool little family guys who even adopt each other's children in the event of an accident. Not only do they not want to suck your blood, they don't want to go near you and will bite you only if they're trapped and you're dumb enough to pick them up. When they hang out at home – and they're entitled to use that phrase – they use some of their non-working time to clean themselves up, so they're not covered in parasites. While they may get rabies, scientists do not regard them as rabies carriers, and humans are immeasurably more likely to catch rabies as a result of a dog bite than from a bat. Experiments have been done to see how bats react when they get in someone's hair, and the indications are that they like it even less than does the human involved and have a remarkable capacity to free themselves and get the hell out of there quickly.

Bats have done humanity many a favour, too, contrary to public perception. In the rain forest, bats perform the same kind of function that bees and birds do: they pollinate and spread seeds so well that they are pivotal to the survival of many species of fruit and vegetables, including avocados, mangoes, peaches, figs and dates.

Studying them has helped the development of aids for people with visual impairment because of the clever way they use sonar. They've also played their part in the development of vaccines and we may need fairly speedily to study their ability to hibernate at will whenever food is in short supply. If a famine happens, some of them can just sleep through it.

Plus they're shy and gentle and fruit bats are quite pretty, looked at the right way.

Now you know all these facts, if you simply have an inchoate fear of the bat population, you will feel less fearful. If, however, you are in a cold sweat and ready to throw up or faint as a result of the information, the chances are that you have a phobia about bats, because one of the distinguishing features of phobia is that it is not amenable to reason. No matter what information is provided, the phobia stays floridly present, generating a number of physical symptoms. Some phobics cannot speak because their throat closes up when they are faced with what they fear. They can't breathe, their mouth goes dry and their heartbeat speeds up. They may perspire profusely, feel physically sick and develop the shakes. They may get light-headed, physically freeze or even faint.

None of which is to suggest that these symptoms are a product of a weird upbringing or some kind of mental disorder. The reality is that fit, confident and optimistic human beings, asked to walk across a plank suspended on scaffolding sixties storeys above the ground, would experience many, if not all of these symptoms, even though their rational brain might remind them that the task requires the same skill as walking across a similar plank suspended on bricks a few millimetres off the ground. (Of course, the rational mind also points out that falling off a plank placed near the ground may result in a twisted ankle, whereas falling from the sixtieth floor will kill you.)

Phobics can choose to cope, even in bizarre ways, with their problem. Actors working for Alfred Hitchcock, to take just one example, would tell each other that the one sure way to drive him out of his mind was to stub out a cigarette in an eggshell, as he was phobic about eggs (suffering from ovophobia) and had a big hatred going against cigarettes. Many phobics are like functioning alcoholics. They manage the circumstances around their phobia so cleverly that few outsiders ever have a clue that they suffer from it.

Eventually the effort of manageing the phobia takes up too much time and energy, or they hate the way it makes them behave, so they decide they have to do something about it. Almost every website devoted to individual phobias provides links to systems, largely based on autosuggestion and repetition, designed to allow someone to rid themselves of their own obsession.

If that doesn't work, a self-help group, personal therapist or participation in a training programme may be possible.

Here's the bottom line.

Fears can be faced up to. Phobias may require avoidance or treatment

For example, Ireland's EU Commissioner, Maire Geoghegan-Quinn, is terrified of birds. Vultures? Yes. Eagles? Definitely. Robins?* Afraid so. Canaries? Them, too. The woman in charge of innovation and research for an entire continent chooses avoidance. She will not enter a house containing a budgie. The fear – according to a column she wrote in *The Irish Times* – is probably rooted in some bad childhood experience. Many people have such fears, but it's not always possible to dig out the traumatic cause.

Nor is digging for childhood roots necessarily helpful. The actor, Anthony Hopkins, had a strange childhood during which he was slow, introverted and listless, convinced that there was something odd about him. He later developed alcoholism and now devotedly attends AA meetings and believes that he is the maker of his own happiness, destiny and good fortune.

'It sounds a rather Thatcherite or kind of callous way of looking at life,' he admits, 'but finally that's it. Get on with it. My creed is get on with it. I'm blessed, I suppose, to find a loophole, to find an escape hatch from the addiction and destructive side of my life. I've found a way into the open air and I don't want ever to look back or to go back. If somebody phones me up and says, "I'm feeling depressed," I say, "Why, are you homeless? Have you got leukaemia?" and if they say,

---

*And don't go, 'Ah, she couldn't be frightened of robins.' Just because they look pretty on Christmas cards, this doesn't mean that robins win anything other than the bird beauty contest. They're viciously territorial. When two of them hitched a ride on a cruise ship, they separated the top deck in two and if one of them crossed the invisible border between territories, the other would half-kill it.

"No", I say, "Well, stop it." They say, "My job is affecting me." I say "Don't let it affect you. Get out of the job or find something, just something positive in life.'"

Fear can be rational or irrational. Either kind can disable by freezing you in position, unable to think for yourself or take action to get you out of the frightening situation. If you ever find yourself in such a situation, or you regularly find yourself there, an ostensibly simple bit of advice is to be found in the bestselling *Who Moved my Cheese?* It takes the form of a question one of the characters in the parable encounters when, starving and fearful, he rounds the corner in a maze he must traverse.

'What would you do if you weren't afraid?' asks the sign.

If you're filled with fear, options seem thin on the ground. Worse, you may not be able to see any of the available options because you become hazard-fixated. That's why asking yourself that question, in any situation where you are fearful, can be useful. If it's unanswerable, if, in other words, you cannot imagine any situation better than the scenario you currently occupy, then you may be at the mercy of a phobia, and, depending on what it is, should seek professional help to address it. If, on the other hand, you can imagine what you would do if you were not afraid, you can teach yourself to 'behave as if.' 'Behaving as if' means acting as you know you would if fear were not crippling you. Your behaviour in any normal situation can come into play.

It's a marvellously freeing question. It can liberate a frightened person to do the right thing, rescue themselves and others in a crisis or back out of a coward's option.

2

Fear of People

Eyes down. It's safer that way. If you don't meet the teacher's eyes, maybe he won't order you to come up to the front of the class and read out what you've written. If you don't meet the chairman's eyes, maybe he won't call on you to contribute to the meeting. If you don't meet the hostess's eyes, maybe she won't pounce on you and drag you off to meet that person she just *knows* you'll love.

Eyes down, breathing shallow, hands writhing around each other. That's how shyness shows in adults. In children, it's the head ducked behind mother's hair or the limbs entwined around father's leg.

Every aspect of social life that is positive for most people is an agony for shy people. The phone call carrying an invitation to have a few drinks with workmates. The email announcing a school reunion. The card telling of an impending birthday party. The request for a date. The instruction to attend a reception. The possibility of making a speech.

Mild shyness is attractive and a matter of a few tentative seconds at the beginning of an encounter with strangers. Serious shyness amounts to social phobia and can result in the shy person opting out of swatches of life that seem like pleasant routine for the rest of us.

Hippocrates summed up the misery of the extreme form of shyness when he described a patient who 'through bashfulness, suspicion and timorousness will not be seen abroad. He dare not come in company, or fear he should be misused, disgraced, overshoot himself in gestures or speeches, or be sick; he thinks every man observes him.'

Social phobia is a major problem for many of its sufferers

in a way it would not have been in previous centuries. In the past, the tongue-tied young lady looking up from under her eyelashes was regarded as particularly fragile and in need of care and sustenance. Indeed, previous times offered recluses an almost professional way to express their lack of interest in socialising. The monks in those beehive stone cells on the Skelligs off the coast of Kerry clearly weren't eager to party. They lived isolated lives devoted to prayer and working on illuminated manuscripts, and they were happy. Not only were they happy, but they were respected, even revered, as, throughout the history of Christianity, were fellows and girls who walked away from family and friends to live on their own or in restricted contact with the rest of the world.

Fear of Commitment: Commitmentphobia

This one isn't a fear at all. The woman who says she has 'commitment issues' really means that she's enjoying her single-with-benefits life far too much to tie herself down with a permanent partner, never mind a couple of kids and a Labrador. Similarly, although his girlfriend may explain away inaction on the part of her guy by telling her VBFs that he has a fear of commitment, (often supposedly generated by the breakup of his parents' marriage and consequent personal trauma) the fact is that he's just not that into her but can't be bothered to sacrifice the support system she provides in order to be totally truthful with himself or her.

Solitude, as a career and life possibility, has almost completely vanished. From the toddler years onward, signs of not wanting to play or share with others are taken to signify a developmental deficit. For example, the child who, in playschool, operates as a sole trader and never speaks is likely to find themselves in front of a therapist. Nor is it safe for an adult to say, 'I've nothing against people but really, I prefer to be on my own.' A couple of hobbies, like long-distance running, permit people to be on their own, but few long-distance runners announce that it's aloneness, rather than fitness and flowing endorphins, that they're after. Greta Garbo's famous line, 'I want to be left alone,' would be almost impossible for any film star to utter, these days, when constant interaction with the fan base through celeb magazines, Facebook and Twitter is *de rigueur* for actors.

The point at which a preference for avoidance of people turned into a problem to be treated was around the beginning of the twentieth century, when a French psychiatrist named Pierre Janet wrote about '*la phobie des situations sociales*' as a problem affecting some of his patients.

Most phobias are rooted in some bad past experience. Social phobia is something of an exception. Shyness, edging into social phobia, is seen as a trait from very early in life. It may even be an inherited trait.

In the 1960s, a psychologist named Jerome Kagan, studying children, realised that, while many babies go through a phase where the sudden arrival of a new face upsets them (so they 'make strange') most get over it within months. However, in some children, shyness went much further than 'making strange'. He began to suspect that the only trait that seemed to stay unchanged from the infant years to adulthood was a shy temperament. As time went on, Kagan became more curious about this 'behaviour inhibition' and picked out two contrasting groups of toddlers. One was made up of sociable, extroverted, talkative two-year-olds. The other was made up of inhibited, shy children of the same age.

Five years later, when the shy children were tested again, the overwhelming majority of them were still inhibited: quiet, serious and more cautious than those in the control group. The same happened when they were tested again five years later. Virtually no child who started out on their life path with a strong tendency towards shyness ever became a bouncy uninhibited teenager.

Jerome Kagan theorised that perhaps the amygdala of

the shy children was more easily activated than that in more socially-comfortable children, so they were always on the verge of flight. Which raised the possibility that the shyness had been present since birth. After all, if it was consistent from the age of two until the mid-teens, it seemed a reasonable assumption that it had been present in the first years of life. So Kagan went even further back, and found that two out of ten children, tested at four months, showed significant distress when subjected to a sudden noise or any unexpected stimulus. They weren't intrigued or entertained by the stimulus. They were inhibited and upset.

Three years later, the 20 per cent of children who had over-reacted to external stimulus turned out to be – yes, you've guessed it – shy. Kagan even went into the womb and was able to indicate that children with a raised heartbeat while still in there were likely to become easily over-stimulated babies and, in turn, shy toddlers.

Finally, he looked at the families of children who were shy and found that the parents of shy toddlers tended themselves to be socially inhibited. So social phobia or shyness runs in families. It doesn't always follow, any more than red hair follows from one generation to the next, but it's an increased likelihood, just as, in the case of identical twins, if one of the pair is a social phobic, there's a one in four chance the other will be, too.

Social phobia appears in most cultures and is widely distributed, but knowing others are in the same pickle doesn't help you if the very thought of dating makes you blush and the thought of eating in front of someone else turns you scarlet. Because one of the giveaways of shyness is blushing.

> *There's a blush for won't, and a blush for shan't*
> *And a blush for having done it.*
> *There's a blush for thought and a blush for nought,*
> *And a blush for just begun it.*

This is what John Keats wrote about blushing and it would seem he found the whole thing rather endearing. From the outside, a blush may be winsome and charming. From the inside, it never is. Being on the inside of a blush means feeling a wave of heat pour up the neck, like the fizz in a bottle of Coke that's been shaken and then uncapped, wash over the face, swell the ears and make the scalp sweat. The only thing worse than the blush itself is the possibility that some fool will draw attention to it.

'Oooh, look at her, she's blushing,' has to be roughly as maddening as what gets said to children: 'Oooh, look, he's shy. You're not shy, are you?' Both comments tend to be delivered at high volume with the speaker's face way too close for comfort.

Charles Darwin seems to have had a severe case of 'Ooooh, look at her, she's blushing.' He studied the phenomenon, being particularly eager to find out how far down the body blushes extended. A doctor pal of his agreed to be his blush spy for a few years, given that Darwin wasn't in much of a position to invite women in embarrassing situations to strip for him at the point of blushing, whereas a female patient in a surgery might find stripping for other procedures sufficiently invasive to generate a blush worth observing.

'He finds,' Darwin reported, after the pal had done three years of extensive study, 'that with women who blush intensely on the face, ears and nape of neck the blush does not commonly extend any lower down the body. It is rare to see it as low down as the collarbones and shoulder blades.'

That wasn't enough for Darwin. He found another blush-watcher, who told him of a case of a little girl, 'shocked by what she imagined to be an act of indelicacy [who] blushed all over her abdomen and the upper parts of her body.'

The only conclusion Darwin seems to have reached, as a result of this exhaustive study, was that blushing is 'the most peculiar and the most human of all expressions.' Mark Twain put it more succinctly. 'Man is the only animal that blushes,' he said. 'Or needs to.'

One of the needs fulfilled by blushing may be subservience. One psychologist has suggested that a blush is the equivalent of a dog rolling over and showing its belly to another dog.

'You're big and powerful and I don't want to fight with you, so you don't have to attack me,' is the canine message sent by the posture and a blush may be the human way of delivering the same message. Which is fine if it applied to all races. Dark-skinned people blush, too, only it can't be seen by a potential attacker, so what's the point?

Chronically shy people worry constantly about the possibility of doing something that would embarrass them. When that something happens, it can change their life. Barbra Streisand is generally regarded as a tough cookie, but she has always suffered from massive stage fright, which is often an aspect of shyness. Her definitive embarrassing moment happened at a live concert in New York's Central Park in the early 1960s. One minute, she was singing a song. The next minute, disaster struck.

'I forgot the words in front of 125,000 people and I wasn't cute about it or anything. I was shocked. I was terrified.'

She didn't do another live performance for twenty-seven years. Now, she could have sought treatment for her social phobia. This treatment tends to start with exploring, with the phobic, how out of kilter is their view of themselves and their performance, measured against the judgement of other people. I find, for example, that when I train a social phobic in, say, performing at meeting or making a presentation, they always rate their DVD poorly, if asked to mark it out of ten. Now, part of this is that social phobics always like to stick the knife into themselves first as a way of warding off external criticism. But even taking this as a given, if I then give the DVD to a group of uninvolved people and ask them to mark it, they tend to rate it as at least above average and sometimes as excellent. What seems to be in play here is a version of body dysmorphia. Just as anorexics, forced to look at their skeletal bodies in a mirror, still manage to perceive themselves as fat, so social phobics, given external evidence that nobody notices what they believe to be obvious, discount the evidence.

'Oh, they're just trying to be nice to me,' they say.

Or they believe the viewers were sorry for them. If someone's social phobia so skews their view of real life, therapy, rather than training, is what they need. If they genuinely want to get over their overwhelming shyness, then, over time, a skilled psychotherapist can help them realise: a) that not everybody is looking at them all of the time – most people don't care that much about them; b) that everybody makes allowances for mistakes and that sometimes, making a mistake can be endearing, rather than hate-inducing; and c) that they are sabotageing themselves by their own internal commentary. The internal commentary is the vulture referred to on pages 41-2. It's the voice that, unbidden, announces, 'You're no good at this. You've never been good at it. This upcoming challenge will be the worst and you will fail at it, yet again.'

The desire to overcome shyness is the key to a successful assault on the problem. If it is a problem. In the 1950s first run of Disney's TV programme, *The Mickey Mouse Club*, one of its teenage stars was Annette Funicello, who couldn't enjoy her teen queen status because of her disabling shyness and who went to Walt Disney, her ultimate boss, begging to see a psychologist. He wouldn't allow it, telling her that her shyness was part of her appeal.

That's fine. Up to a point. The point is the line at which the shy person makes decisions that can either make their life easier or lay down serious limitations. Training yourself or going for therapy are decisions that can make your life easier. Deciding to avoid pointlessly embarrassing encounters is another option.

Take this example of a married woman in her late twenties. Let's call her Tess. Tess and her husband are set to go to a big corporate dinner. An hour before they're due to leave, she is trying on the third dress and deciding that it's even worse than the first two. She's regretting that she's teetotal, because a stiff gin would remove the terror currently causing her hands to moisten and her insides to pleat. She knows that she will be rigid with tension throughout the evening, terrified of overturning a glass or failing to remember a name.

Then she notices that her husband is leaning up against the wall, laughing at her.

'What's funny?' she demands, checking to see what's wrong with her clothes.

He smiles silently at her, maddening her even more.

'Tess, you don't have to go,' he tells her. 'There's no law you're going to break if you don't turn up. You don't have to go to any party, reception or anything else. Ever.'

'What about you?'

'I'll go on my own if I feel like it. If I don't, I won't.'

She hugged him, stripped off the third dress, wiped off the make-up, slipped into pyjamas and got into bed. Thereafter, she never went to any dinner party with more than two additional guest couples and eschewed all other social events. Very few people noticed (she clearly hadn't been much of a draw in the first place) and she lived a much happier life.

How do I know? Because I am that woman. My husband puts on his tuxedo and his dicky bow and goes off to socialise without me. When people ask why I'm not with him, he tells them I'm shy. They think he's nuts, because I appear on TV and radio, make speeches and chair conferences. But all of those things are *performances* where taking care of other people is the objective: giving value to a radio audience, entertaining people after a celebratory dinner or making sure a conference runs briskly and informatively. Put me in a situation where I have to introduce or interview someone, even in front of a thousand people, and, although I'll be properly nervous, I won't be an aphasic, amnesic, blithering wreck.

If you can control your exposure to truly terrifying events

or venues without its doing your career or your life any damage, it's sensible to do so. However, many shy people limit their exposure to so many encounters that the quality of their work life and private life deteriorates. Many people with social phobia fail to get the jobs or promotions they should, some do less well in the educational system than their intellectual capacity would suggest would be within their range, and some end up socially isolated.

'Adults with social phobia,' say Schneier and Welkowitz, 'have been consistently shown to have lower rates of marriage than would otherwise be expected.'

If your shyness is of that degree, think seriously about taking charge of it, so that it doesn't own and restrict you and your life.

3

Fear of Optimism

At first glance, it may seem peculiar to suggest that optimism is something of which anybody could be fearful. The reality, however, is that the economic destruction of the past few years has created a situation where even the most instinctively positive people fear to express their optimism. For fear they'll be proven wrong. For fear they will seem unwise. For fear they may draw the Fates down upon them. It could be suggested that, right now, optimism should come with a health warning attached: being buoyant and sunny will make you seem shallow, unsophisticated and too thick to understand how bad things really are.

It has ever been thus. In *Candide*, a book that topped the bestseller lists in 1759, Voltaire created a tutor for Candide, named Dr Pangloss, who had a laser-like focus on the positive.

'All is for the best in the best of all possible worlds,' was his theme. (Obviously, this was a wee while before the property bubble burst and the Celtic Tiger got mange.)

No bitching. No moaning. No blame game. You'd think he'd have been the hero of the book but Voltaire put him in so that he could use him as a punch bag. Imagine inventing someone just to diss him. This says much more about the author than it does about the character.

Optimistic characters have, of course, surfaced in real life, and in their own time, either made a lot of money out of their positive attitudes or became famous, then or later. Forty years ago, a favourite question in radio quizzes was 'Who said, "Every day, in every way, I'm getting better and better."?' The answer was Émile Coué.

Coué would have driven Voltaire straight up every available wall. Coué was a bright man who first studied psychology and then became a pharmacist in his native Brittany.

As a pharmacist – they were then called apothecaries – Coué discovered what would later be dubbed 'the placebo effect'. This happens when clinical trials of a new drug are conducted, with neither the patient nor the doctor knowing whether the patient is getting the new drug or a capsule filled with sugar. The trials sometimes discover that the new drug isn't worth a toss. They sometimes prove (to wild cries of delight from the pharmaceutical company) that the new drug is a killer. A killer in the positive sense. But setting all that aside, what most of these clinical trials prove is that the placebo – the pill that actually has no drug in it at all, good, bad or indifferent – works for a certain portion of the patients being tested. It seems that, because these patients believe they're taking something effective, they get better, even though what they're getting has no pharmacological effect whatsoever.

Coué worked the placebo effect very cleverly, telling his patients that the remedy he made up for them was exceptionally effective. He realised that the patients given this validation did markedly better than those to whom he said nothing and he figured that they were doing something close to hypnosis on themselves. So he studied with expert hypnotists before setting up the Lorraine Society of Applied Psychology, which was devoted to training people in self-hypnosis.

'This is an instrument that we possess at birth, and with which we play unconsciously all our life, as a baby plays with its rattle,' he wrote. 'It is however a dangerous instrument; it can wound or even kill you if you handle it imprudently and unconsciously. It can on the contrary save your life when you know how to employ it consciously.'

'Imprudent and unconscious' use of auto-suggestion would be where the individual allows a negative idea to squat in their brain and inform all their thinking and action. The reverse was his own system, where the person said this 'Every day in every way' mantra first thing in the morning, several times, as if it were a psychological dumbbell, and did the same thing before they went to bed. The positive idea took root in the brain, according to his theory, and would eventually become an external reality. It wouldn't work with some daft unrealistic ambition but if the objective was within the range of possibilities, Coué's method made it more likely to eventuate. If you'd had a leg amputated, you wouldn't regrow the limb, but if you tended to get hay-fever, you could reduce how often you sniffled.

This relentlessly positive approach to illness was later to extend to cancer sufferers, with the promise that if they stayed positive, they might beat their illness. Which had the downside of making patients whose disease recurred feel like failures, because they believed they hadn't been sufficiently optimistic. Some evidence has been found, though, to suggest that being optimistic can reduce your chance of suffering a stroke. A study at the University of Michigan looked at six thousand people over fifty who had not, at the point where the study began, experienced a stroke. The researchers rated the optimism levels of participants on a sixteen-point scale and then observed what became of them. After a two-year period, what emerged was that eighty-eight people had suffered strokes – but that each one point increase in optimism brought a 9 per cent decrease in stroke risk. So the early positive thinkers had something going for them.

Although Coué, even before scientific evidence supported his determined positivity, clearly owned a useful insight, Europe, being old-world and cynical, never took it up the way the Americans did.

Signs on it, even Pollyanna, the title character in Eleanor Porter's early-twentieth-century children's books, was American. This kid – played in the Disney movie by a fourteen-year-old Hayley Mills – was the orphaned daughter of missionaries who was sent to live with an aunt and who, because she was able to find the good in any situation, transformed the town where the aunt resided. Pollyanna and her positivity had a good run for a while but then cynicism poisoned her well and her name became synonymous with infuriating chirpiness. Pity. Pollyanna never had a heel-drumming tantrum in the cereal aisle of Tesco. If we could get children to follow her example, parenting would be so much easier and more pleasant.

Fear of Motivational Posters

'For the last two decades,' some anonymous truth teller has observed, 'motivational posters have inflicted unimaginable suffering on the workplaces of the world.'

Adults undeterred by the fading of the Pollyanna brand – particularly if they lived in America, the home of boosterism – fell gladly on books like Norman Vincent Peale's *The Power of Positive Thinking*, and Dale Carnegie's *How to Win Friends and Influence People*. Both have sold millions of copies. If the very idea of the Dale Carnegie approach makes you queasy, this proves you are sophisticated, cynical – and probably ignorant. In fact, Carnegie's book is a lot more than simple-minded salesmanship hype. One of his basic principles is that we do better when we pay more attention to other people than to ourselves. He's right. One of his key pieces of advice, not that he'd put it this bluntly, is: 'Shut up and listen.' He's right. The more you listen to other people, the wiser they think you are. The more interesting you find other people, the more interesting you become. The more you expect each day to be filled with good stuff, the more you view what you encounter, on any given day, as positive and enlightening.

Laughing helps too. Even when you have developed a serious and painful illness, laughter has more to offer than you might have thought. As Norman Cousins, the journalist, found. The prognosis – that he would quickly die of his diagnosed heart disease – was not his worst problem. He was in enormous pain, which, at the time, his doctors were not able to ameliorate. He tried everything, including playing old Marx Brothers movies to himself. Amazingly, the comedy helped.

'I made the joyous discovery that ten minutes of genuine belly laughter had an anaesthetic effect and would give me at least two hours of pain-free sleep,' he wrote.

Cousins lived for more than twenty-five years longer than had been predicted, and used that extra time to develop what has been called 'the biology of hope,' which concentrated on non-traditional methods of coping with dire diagnoses and the symptoms of lethal diseases. Orthodox medicine has always been wary of his theories, despite considerable supportive evidence for them. Undoubtedly, the biology of hope has its downsides, not least of which is the pressure on those who practice it. Cousins, nonetheless, changed some of the assumptions around terminal illness. He did it through extensive controlled studies and through even more extensive talking and writing about the topic.

So whether you want to prevent illness, manage pain or develop your career, it's a good idea to find ways to be cheerful and to laugh.

If you do it consistently, you might even overcome the human tendency, revealed again and again by research, to place a lot more value on negative than on positive information.

According to American writer Paul Waldman, a good reason lies behind the greater attention we pay to bad news. 'The explanation from evolutionary psychology,' he maintains, 'is that looking out for danger was essential to survival (ignore a tasty raspberry bush and you'll go hungry for a day; ignore a saber-toothed tiger and you won't be passing on your genes).

As the political scientists Michael Cobb and James Kuklinski put it, voters 'assign relatively more weight and importance to events that have negative, as opposed to positive, implications for them or those dear to them. When making decisions, they place more emphasis on avoiding potential losses than on obtaining potential gains. Similarly, when individuals form impressions of situations of other people, they weight negative information more heavily than positive...Impressions formed on the basis of negative information, moreover, tend to be more lasting and more resistant to change.'

Those impressions are likely to be external and of other people. Because (step up, Pollyanna), Martin Seligman, founder of the positive-psychology movement, finds that happy people remember more good events in their lives than actually occurred, whereas depressed people remember the past as it actually happened. Which doesn't improve their current mood one little bit. There's a case for the 'Every day, in every way, I'm getting better and better' type of self-delusion.

If Pollyanna had been a boy, she'd have grown up to be Professor Martin Seligman of the University of Pennsylvania, a past President of the American Psychological Association. Seligman did a fascinating experiment a few years back, when he persuaded an insurance company to allow him to pick a team of salespeople to work alongside the team the HR people within the company had recruited that year. The insurance firm, understandably, had recruited salespeople who were highly qualified, highly educated and experienced. Seligman just picked people who were optimistic. He handed them a questionnaire, and if their responses showed them to be adult Pollyannas, they had the job – never mind if they had neither previous experience nor a relevant degree.

When the company's end of financial year came around, the results of the two teams were measured against each other and Seligman's team of bright-and-bushy-tailed folk beat the others. They didn't just do a bit better than the others. They knocked hell out of them. Exceeded their sales by 21 per cent in year one and 57 per cent in year two, thus supporting Seligman's theory that optimism tends to lead to greater sales.

Nor does he confine this productivity claim to selling alone. It applies in almost all areas of business.

Coué and others showed that, by constant reinforcement of yourself, it is possible to embrace that feared trait, optimism, and make it work for you. He realised that, while negativity is always tempting and tends to make the person expressing it seem realistic and wise, positivity actually works. If people get over their fear of seeming naively hopeful.

It's all about choice. Well, actually, it's not. Genetics, circumstances and internal chemistry also play their part. But we can indubitably make choices for ourselves or in the way we raise our children that have an impact on our level of optimism or that of our children, and one of those choices, which has a decidedly negative impact, is to buy into the self-esteem craze. According to Professor Seligman, the focus on raising self-esteem, which is supposed to make people feel good, in fact results in them becoming depressed.

'Self-esteem emphasis has made millions think there's something fundamentally wrong if you don't feel good, as opposed to just "'I don't feel good right now, but I will later,"' Seligman says.

At any given time of any given day, even the most buoyant of personalities may not feel wonderful about life, the universe and themselves. It's normal, and anybody who maintains that everybody should expect to feel good about themselves all the time is doing no good at all for anyone they may advise, because they're setting up as the norm a set of expectations which are completely unrealistic.

Anyone who wants to become more optimistic, or who finds that they can't get a grip on the pessimism that overwhelms them, can find a cognitive therapist or learn from the principles of that kind of therapy.

'If you want to improve your mood, energy and optimism, you have to start by analysing what you say to yourself. If, when things in your life go wrong, or are not as you would like them to be, your internal monologue is preoccupied with blaming yourself, and in particular finding fault with yourself, then you may be suffering from a bad case of ANTs,' according to psychiatrist Dr Raj Persaud.

ANTs? Automatic Negative Thoughts. The personal coinage of Dr Persaud. Automatic Negative Thoughts are like a vulture permanently affixed to your shoulder. The vulture on your shoulder talks to you all the time but particularly during periods of stress, like when you're making a speech or involved in a contentious meeting. The vulture mutters judgements on what you're doing and the judgements are always negative. 'Made a mess of that, didn't you?' it will say. 'And you're going to make a mess of the next bit, too. Just watch.'

Most people who acknowledge having a vulture say that it talks in their mother's voice. As a mother, I wish to reject this as a vile slur on motherhood, but it does hark back to some research that was done involving fitting three-year-olds with recorders that picked up everything said to the children over a couple of weeks, with the aim of getting an objective measure of the messages sent to kids by adults. 85 per cent of them turned out to be negative. All instructions as to what they were not to do or criticisms of what they'd just done. According to Persaud, psychologists and psychiatrists believe that these repeated negatives coming at us during our formative years 'are probably incorporated into our outlook on life, in the form of self-talk – what we say to ourselves during our continuous inner conversation.'

Some people, those who are natural optimists, don't have a vulture. They have a sort of in-built cheerleader, who tells them they're playing a blinder. Since every thought you have affects your mood, it follows that the more you can move away from vulture and towards cheerleader, the better you'll feel about the world.

'The solution is to become aware of these negative judgements and labels you automatically use to describe yourself, and to replace each devaluing statement with a more objective description of yourself,' says Persaud.

Easy? No. Possible? Yes – with persistence. Hourly, daily, persistence. Because nobody ever replaced a bad habit with a good one without repeating the desired habit so often that it became a reflex.

Worth doing, though. Unless, that is, you want to be or already are a lawyer. Apparently lawyers, as a group, tend to be pessimistic. In fact, law would seem to be the great exception, the one profession where pessimists do better than optimists. One of the theories seeking to explain this is that lawyers are subject to enormous demands but have limited choices. They're at the mercy of precedent, they're at the mercy of testy judges, they've no control over which judge they get and their clients are almost never satisfied.

Whether you are a lawyer or a salesperson, the one thing of which you cannot afford to be afraid is optimism. Sophistication may lie in following Voltaire and sneering at cheery folk who genuinely believe that everything's going to turn out well. Personal and career progress, however, may lie in the possibility of overcoming fear of optimism. You may not look at yourself in the mirror and tell your reflection that every day in every way, you're getting better and better, but it's a hell of an improvement on listening to the vulture on your shoulder who predicts that every day in every way, you're failing more egregiously.

4

Fear of Ridicule

Fear of ridicule has always existed. Now, social media has brought ridicule out of the shadows and turned individual begrudgers into an electronic mob, capable of doing a level of collective damage they could never have delivered, isolated from each other. McLuhan's global village frequently manifests itself in remote-control graffiti-writing about individuals. De-friending someone, sharing horrible pictures of them or retweeting nasty comments about them are all options for anybody who wants to take someone else down a peg or three.

The methods are new and handy. The reflex is as old as time.

In ancient Rome, as soon as anybody became powerful, satirists would immediately set out to prevent them getting above themselves, issuing commentaries about their looks, lisps and lame excuses. Male VIPs, even Caesar, were frequently mocked for their baldness and their attempts to conceal it. One devastating poem talks of a balding man filling in the gaps by drawing ink lines on his scalp.

Tolstoy said that Napoleon feared *le ridicule* more than anything else in the world. Some would suggest that the grandiloquence of his vision and the tragedy of the attack on and retreat from Moscow all derived from the fear of being mocked and derided for his mistakes.

The more totalitarian the regime, the less ridicule is permitted. No doubt residents of the old USSR thought Stalin ridiculous, but the promise of a trip to the Gulag would have dampened down their desire to say so in public. Alexander Solzhenitsyn, a Red Army officer, was hardly back from World

War II when he was transported to Siberia because he had said something critical of Stalin and the politburo in a letter home from the front. Similarly, in Hitler's Germany, anybody who said anything satirical about the Führer was effectively booking their passage to a concentration camp.

In free democracies, pouring ridicule on our betters is an essential strand of our culture. Not because our rulers are necessarily any more open to being mocked than are/were dictators, but because few of them have a Gulag handy. Ireland has a strong satirical tradition, whereby writers mock the best efforts (and the worst efforts) of those at the top. Going back to the writings of Jonathan Swift, the Dean of St Patrick's, it's clear that the main objective of writings like *Gulliver's Travels* was not to entertain children but to change the government policies of the day, through ridicule.

More recently, a shrugging resignation was the response to programmes like *Hall's Pictorial Weekly* and *Scrap Saturday*. Such programmes might rename a politician 'The Minister for Hardship,' or portray a Taoiseach's adviser, like P.J. Mara vis-a-vis Charlie Haughey, as a craven moron, but neither P.J. nor the ministers involved took offence. Indeed, Michael Noonan made no secret of enjoying the portrayal of him on *Scrap Saturday* as a cute conspiratorial hoor. What is amazing is to find the same man mocked and mimicked on *Nob Nation* and *Gift Grub*, twenty years later.

Writers have always ridiculed politicians. But long before they got around to politicians, writers – going back to Aristophanes in Ancient Greece – ridiculed each other whenever they got a public opportunity. In medieval times, it happened as part of a festival, with poets competing to say the most outrageous things about each other.

In more modern times, the best opportunity for dissing another writer, even if they're: a) well-established, e'en to the point of critical impregnability; or b) dead, is offered by an invitation to review their work. George Bernard Shaw hated Shakespeare with a passion.

'Pure melodrama,' he wrote of *Hamlet* in 1897. 'There is not a touch of characterisation that goes below the skin.'

Samuel Pepys and Voltaire agreed with Shaw. Having seen a production of *A Midsummer Night's Dream* in London in 1662, Pepys described it as 'the most insipid, ridiculous play that I ever saw in my life.' Voltaire believed Shakespeare wouldn't be tolerated in France or Italy and suggested *Hamlet* was 'the work of a drunken savage'.

None of which bothered Shakespeare that much, as he was profoundly dead at the time all three rubbished his work. However, the book review offers hate-filled writers an opportunity to rubbish the work of someone they know or at least with whom they share a period of time.

Many take up this cudgel with great willingness, on the basis, as Edna St Vincent Millay put it, that 'a person who publishes a book wilfully appears before the populace with his pants down…If it is a good book, nothing can hurt him. If it is a bad book, nothing can help him.' Which is a neatly pleasing way of articulating a patent untruth. Any writer who has ever received a drubbing at the hands of even the most obscure critic remembers that review all their lives, long after the good ones have leached out of their memory.

More to the point, a bad review can destroy, not the book, but the writer. Herman Melville was mortified into artistic silence for thirty years by reviewers and history doesn't bother to record the number of first-time novelists who never venture into print again, following the savageing of their baby. The reviewers may be right, although Kurt Vonnegut said he could never understand reviewers getting vicious about a novel. It seemed to him roughly the equivalent of getting fully dressed in armour and mounting a horse carrying a spear in order to attack an ice-cream cone.

If you are an aspiring writer, you must remember that other writers don't always get it right. They may be fine writers themselves but it doesn't follow that their judgement of others will be meritorious. Dr Johnson, for example, condemned the poetry of John Donne, while Henry James had no time for Emily Brontë.

When you've written your book and it is published, you cannot control the reviewers. Yes, it's true, some reviewers deliberately seek the opportunity to have a go at a writer they hate. Now and then, however, the opposite happens. How about this as a review in the *San Juan County Record* of Edward Abbey's *The Monkey Wrench Gang*: 'The author of this book should be neutered and locked away forever.' Except that the review was written by the author himself, who clearly has a sense of humour and an understanding that even a God-awful review can sell books.

What is infinitely painful is when a writer you like and who likes you and may even be a friend dismisses your work as a stinker. Thomas More got so maddened by a bad review that he turned it into a matter of life and death, challenging the reviewer to a duel. Luckily for both men, the law arrived in time to stop them killing each other.

Paul Theroux's review of Erica Jong's *Fear of Flying*, published in 1974, was devastating: 'This crappy novel,' he said, 'misusing vulgarity to the point where it becomes purely foolish, picturing women as a hapless organ animated by the simplest ridicule, and devaluing imagination in every line... represents everything that is to be loathed in American fiction today.'

Jong says the review, back then, broke her heart. However, as the book is now a classic with ten million copies in print in languages ranging from Japanese to Serbo-Croat, she admits the review doesn't have the personal sting it once had. Ten million copies sold would anaesthetise the misery a bit, all right. Every writer wants unanimous critical acclaim plus bestseller status. Few get it. Most, sooner or later, get a critical evisceration and a book that doesn't sell. But they wrote it. It was published. They had, for one bright shining moment, the thrill of holding it in their hand the book. None of which they'd have had if they'd been terrified into silence by the prospect of reviewer ridicule.

The march of folly we laughingly call human progress is dotted with idiot decisions made out of a desire to avoid personal ridicule or persevered with for the same reason. The advance of what we laughingly call 'social' media allows ridicule to be delivered in real time and experienced by iPad, smartphone and computer. Never has it ever been so easy to learn just what a plank other people believe you to be.

Twitter is where some of the most toe-curling abuse is to be found. Tweets come in two types. Banalities from the rich and famous. And pure venom from the poor and unknown who have been bypassed by life, and who sit ready to react poisonously and anonymously to anybody who does or says anything. These folk are like individual volcanoes, filled with bile, ready to overflow.

Former tweeters like Ryan Tubridy have learned to their cost that the people who follow them will turn on them in a split second, in a way that real friends never do.

It's always been possible to reach into the lives of famous people to torment and jeer them. Marilyn Monroe said that being famous permitted people to be rude to you in a way they never would, if you weren't a household name and an instantly identifiable face.

Now, however, it's possible to reach into the lives of people who are not famous, particularly those of teenagers. No matter how loving the relationship with parents, every teenager has secrets they cannot share with their mother and father because they know their parents will never understand. Not really.

Adults develop merciful amnesia for just how vicious schoolmates were in their time. From the distance of decades, they make reassuring noises that these bullies don't matter, must have no lives. But, to the teenager being tortured, those reassurances are no more than noises. Prophecies that in some future time the torturers will be forgotten have no reality. The misery is now, as is the terror of the electronic mob and the skewering agony of reading and rereading cruelties in print.

Today, if you are a teenager, you are at the mercy of any digital bully who wants to take their unhappiness out on you by ridiculing you. You have to hold close to you the few – the very few – people who would die for you and who know you for what you are, you have to define yourself for yourself, and you have to kick the habit of visiting and revisiting Internet torture chambers. They'll continue to say things behind your back? So? Time to get the resolution to mutter to yourself, as you turn off your computer and head out for a run, 'They say. What say they? Let them say...'

Ridicule is the least of your worries if you engage in Facebook. Several careers have come to a juddering halt because people confided their opinions of someone else to a Facebook account restricted to close friends. In one such case, the person who had opined, to their own detriment, asked for my post-factum help. What they'd written about a third party was posted on an open and highly popular site roughly five minutes after they posted it on their own. They couldn't believe that a friend would so speedily do them wrong, although speed wasn't at the core of the problem. What was at the core of the problem was that they seriously believed they owned sixty friends. Nobody does. However, because this person had only sixty friends, and since it's widely known that the average Facebook user has a-hundred-and-thirty friends, they may actually have kidded themselves that the relatively small number with access to their page meant that they were real friends. Not so. It's worth remembering, any time you get the urge to be reckless on Facebook, in the belief that your friends would never do you down, that Benjamin Franklin once opined that three people can keep a secret – if two of them are dead.

While we're on the subject of the Mafia, think about what happened to Salvatore D"Avino, a mobster from the Neapolitan Camorra who went on the run and managed to stay below Interpol radar for more than a decade, at which point his girlfriend posted pictures of herself on Facebook, said pictures taken outside an upscale Marbella nightclub. Aha, said the cops and swarmed on Marbella. End of Sal's freedom.

It's not just the forces of the law who read Facebook. HR people recruiting for staff do. So the student who shares his view that eight pints a night makes him a social drinker may find, when he has graduated, that his CVs don't get quite the response he might have hoped for.

Around the world at the moment, data protection authorities are trying to come to grips with what employers (and potential employers) should do about accessing information about individuals from social media sites.

One American employment lawyer recommends that companies should have a four-pillar policy about social media.

- The business must take reasonable steps to be accurate.
- The employee or candidate should be informed and consent to the background check.
- The employee or candidate must be informed of any adverse action taken as a result of the background check.
- The business should have a policy on how the employee or candidate can challenge the findings or their accuracy.

In the UK, an organisation called Acas (Advisory, Conciliation and Arbitration Service), which resolves employment disputes, has urged employers not to be heavy-handed in the way they may respond to employees putting negative comments (especially about their employer) on their Facebook site. Acas points out that the employer wouldn't, at night, go to the pub to listen in on what employees say or punish them as a result, so why would they use Facebook for the same purpose.

This followed the sacking of an Argos employee who came back from holiday and whined on his Facebook page that deliveries hadn't been done and that he'd come back to 'a bit of a tip'.

'Back to the shambles that is work,' he observed.

Of course he'd have said the same thing over a drink in the local. But the number of people to be found in the average pub who are prepared to listen to, remember and repeat to others any individual's complaints about their workplace is reasonably small, whereas the number of people who might access the same individual's Facebook account and pass on his ridicule would be immeasurably more.

Bottom line: before you put anything on your Facebook page, work out how you would feel if someone showed it to your mother or your boss.

A few lines on Facebook's facial recognition technology. If a photo of you has been uploaded and your name appears alongside that photo, Facebook refers to this as 'tagging'. Ironically, the fear of ridicule forces some Facebook users to stay connected.

Facebook's facial recognition technology continually scans through the albums of all your 'friends' to pick you out of a crowd. Provided you've been 'tagged' in one photo, the software will carry out a full-scale search for other photos in which you appear.

For reluctant Facebook users, ignorance is not bliss. In an image-conscious world, being unable to prevent less than flattering images of you being circulated is a scary thought.

5

Fear of Holidays

Until recently, the number of holidays taken by families each year was a big problem for teachers. When school came back in January, several children would be missing, because of the family skiing holiday. Easter got stretched at the beginning or end in order to take advantage of off-peak fares. Class numbers were depleted in early June for the same reason: get to Orlando before the crowds of other Irish people. Then there was the stretched-out mid-term break in the autumn. It all added up to a situation where a teacher was constantly revising material with those who had been away, while irritating the hell out of the pupils who had been present all the time.

Now, some people are afraid to take holidays at all, whereas in the old days when holidays happened at the same time for everyone, holidays were a joyful release from the normal grind. Choice was not much of an issue. You went to foreign places if you were rich or had relatives there; you went to a seaside hotel or caravan if you couldn't afford air flights; or you might stay at home and go to the beach a lot. The one thing you didn't ever do was go to work. Indeed, those were the days when, if you were lucky enough to work in a bank, failure to go on holiday lit up a red light in your manager's head that perhaps you might have got a little of the bank's money mixed up with your own and were afraid to leave your till in case your replacement found out what you'd been at and how you'd funded your trips to the bookie's shop around the corner.

These days, that fear of taking a holiday has spread way beyond erring bank officials. Increasing numbers of workers here and elsewhere just transfer the day job to a different location and time zone. More sunshine, less sleep, because if a client rings you at nine, their time, it may be three or four in the morning, your time. Interestingly, callers tend to note the funny overseas tone on a mobile phone, but rightly figure that if you pick up, you're on the job. Which, of course, you are, feeling put-upon, indispensable and deeply virtuous.

Last year I watched a woman in a bikini walking at the water's edge of a beach in Florida, totally focused on her mobile phone conversation. Sometimes she'd stop, the waves dribbling over her bare feet, and concentrate, her hand shielding her closed eyes as she tried to visualise what the person on the other line was talking about. Sometimes she'd gesture, as if her auditors were in front of her. Phrases floated past, truncated by the shouts of children and the crunch on sand of arriving cars.

'Impact of cost-cutting,' was one of those phrases.

'The figures from Hutchens, Kansas. They need to be worked up,' was another.

It's tempting to throw a pity party for this holidaymaker who clearly could not cut the electronic umbilical cord to her office and have a *real* holiday. Except for two reasons. The first is that she was clearly having a great time. She was as tuned into the rhythms and themes coming through her tiny phone as – fifteen years ago – kids on the same beach would have been tuned into the rap coming from the ghetto-blasters on their shoulders.

The second reason to withhold sympathy from this woman is that she personifies a significant trend: the electronic abolition of the summer holiday. Years ago, staying in touch with home – never mind the office – during an overseas holiday required carefully coordinated phone calls from a hotel. Holidaymakers exchanged stories of how they'd been overcharged for three-minute conversations.

TV and radio tended to be only in the language of the host country. I remember, in those years, my husband listening to an Italian radio station in the belief that his knowledge of Latin would allow him to understand the news bulletin. He muttered that he thought the Pope might have died.

'The Pope died last month,' I pointed out.

'Yeah, but I think the new one has died, now,' he said, and he was right.

Most hotels in Europe now carry channels in English. In addition, many holiday-makers carry iPads, iPhones or laptops with them and – because of the proliferation of electronic 'hot spots' – can access email and news websites in coffee shops and airports at the drop of a keystroke. And they do. Particularly if they're important in their business.

'For the first time in history, ' David Brooks observes in *On Paradise Drive*, 'people at the top of the income ladder work longer hours than people at the bottom. Over the past twenty years, the proportion of American managers and professionals who work over fifty hours a week has increased by a third.'

Managers and professionals, the very people who, at least in theory, have control over the number of hours they work, are choosing to work longer than they have to and much longer than people at other times and in other places who had no choice about it.

'If we compare our employment patterns with the workday of a hunter-gatherer in the Peruvian forests (three to four hours), the average work week in prerevolutionary France (four days), or the annual number of work-free days in fourth-century Rome (a hundred and seventy-five), we seem a very hard-driven lot,' says anthropologist Margaret Visser.

Irish people, particularly those who buy into the idea of work-life balance, are self-conscious about choosing to work longer hours, but they're doing it, nonetheless, and staying in constant contact with the office even when they're on annual leave. They're doing so in the teeth of reproving glances and comments about workaholics shortening their own life spans. ('Workaholic' is the term of abuse often applied to people who love their work by people who hate their work.)

Work is where we spend the bulk of our life and where we weave essential strands of personal identity and self-worth. On the other hand, the increasingly porous boundary between work and holidays – the fear of shutting down and taking a 'real' unplugged vacation, may be good neither for our health nor our productivity

If you're South Korean, not only do you work an average of 2250 hours a year – at least four hundred more than we do in this part of the world – but you get just eleven days annual leave. Up to now, South Koreans didn't bother much with taking those eleven days in one chunk. They sprinkled their time off throughout the year, apparently because of the workplace culture where wage slaves are afraid that if you go on a holiday and aren't missed, this will be taken as evidence that you weren't really necessary in the first place.

Increasingly, however, employers in that busy part of the world are insisting that their people take real holidays, rather than long weekends throughout the year, and that they don't sneak into the company's computers by long distance while they're away. The Shinhan Financial Group in Seoul, for example, has brought in a system that prevents their people from accessing the computer network at work while they're on vacation.

Shinhan Financial Group would be a bit exceptional, in this. A global survey just published by Robert Half, a recruitment company, found that huge numbers of people in countries, including Chile, Russia, Hungary and Poland, where staff work longer hours than people in western Europe, also tend to link up with work via the internet when they're ostensibly on holiday.

They may do it because they're bored on holiday. They may do it because work is their addiction – remember Noel Coward's comment that 'work is more fun than fun'? Or they may do it as a way of managing their bosses' expectations, since those who stay connected would appear to be in lockstep with employer demands.

'People from Singapore and Hong Kong were regularly connected to work during their vacation time,' a spokesman for the recruitment firm said. 'And over 90 per cent of employers expected their employees to be available and connected during their holiday period.'

Now, we all know that Singapore is a model of productivity, has no chewing gum on its streets, and generally ticks like a clock. But the interesting thing is that South Korea, where they work at least as hard and are entitled to less than half the annual leave accorded to workers in Singapore, has an appalling productivity rate. The BBC says it's one of the lowest among OECD members.

That's the productivity issue. But then there's the health issue. According to a book entitled *The Way We're Working Isn't Working*, a twenty-year study of working women found that the ones who took fewest vacations were twice as likely to get a heart attack as those who took the most.

'Overall, infrequent vacationers had a twenty per cent higher risk of dying from any cause,' says the book's author, Tony Schwartz.

Maybe, in the interests of productivity and survival, more of us should follow the example of people whose phones and emails, once they've gone on holiday, deliver no contact beyond a message saying this is an automatic response because they've taken their bucket and spade and won't be back until a stated date.

These are the folks who have their work/life in balance, whose Labrador is in a good kennel and who don't worry about roaming charges because they even turn off their mobile phone. They don't click on Breakingnews.ie every five minutes while they're away. Nor do they buy newspapers from home while overseas. They shut down. Abandon ship. Forget the workaday world. Devote themselves to recreation. Rediscovery and recovery from the tough year they've had. They are healthy, integrated, sensible. They have their priorities right. You have to hate them.

But you also have to admit that they're healthily free of the fear of taking real holidays.

6

Fear of Change: Neophobia

The writer Maya Angelou has said that you can tell a lot about a person's capacity to handle change by how they react to: a) a wet day; b) lost luggage; c) tangled Christmas tree lights.

When I work with groups on the issue of change, I often start there, by asking individuals for their typical responses to each of the three possibilities. The results are riotous. The most unlikely people recount stories of complete meltdown in the face of lost luggage. Gentle folk turn out have a violent hatred of the umbrella style of others. ('Dear God, the ones who just put their umbrella in front of them and proceed as if they were mandated to kill all before them.') And the tangled Christmas tree lights scenario tends to segment groups straight down the middle, one half admitting to balling the green flex up and throwing it into the wheelie bin, the other half looking scandalised at their lack of patience.

The styles revealed by the Angelou exercise carry through into the attitude to change manifested by the same individuals. Some get focused on obstructions – like the battering-ram umbrella-bearers. Some throw tantrums. Some get defeated. Some – like those who toss the problematic Christmas tree lights – quickly analyse the situation, do a cost-benefit tot in their head and move on.

Another exercise I do is to set two competing groups from within the wider number the task of identifying the body and verbal language that characterises resistance to change. They set to with a will. If they start with the verbals, they come back with sometimes overlapping lists of quotations like:

- 'We tried that twice before and it didn't work then. Why would it work now?'
- 'Every time management brings in consultants, they come up with hairbrained stuff like this.'
- 'Whenever they tell you not to be afraid of change, you know it's code for 'work harder for less money'.
- 'Last time we went on a change course, we got to shoot red ink at each other in a wood. What stupid game are we going to have to play, this time?'
- 'Does the shop steward know about this?'
- 'How come it's always the troops on the ground who have to change, and never the top guys?'
- 'Ah, yeah. The new flavour of the month.'
- 'I've read the cheese book. Puhlease.'

The groups laugh as they compare and contrast their lists. But they quickly get into discussion about how frequently the comments are justified – it is possible, for example, that a particular 'new' approach to the business has been tried before, and has failed, yet once the tide of change flows through an organisation, anyone who points to this fact may get labelled as a change resister who is 'being defensive'. Which, of course, forces them even further on to the defensive.

Classic examples of change-avoidance language include the vague and personal: 'I'm not sure I'd be comfortable with that,' and a tendency to move away from the specific to the general. It's the job of a good manager gently to rule out emotional statements and seek, instead, the evidence supporting a belief that a proposed change will not work. It's also the job of a good manager to bring people back to specific proposals, rather than allow fearful generalised verbal wandering.

Given a little prompting, groups quickly become highly skilled at identifying negative language and finding ways to avoid inadvertently employing the patois of pessimism. The reflex needed is a kind of three-phase process:

- 'We won't be able to do X because of Y.' (Extreme pessimism – a change disabler)
- 'We won't be able to do X unless we have Y.' (Pessimism)
- 'If we got Y, we could do X.' (Optimism)

This is important, because pessimists carry enormous negative power. They tend to be regarded, at times of change, as realists. But their power is arguably best illustrated by what happened following the publication of Goethe's *The Sorrows of Young Werther,* about a clinically depressed suicide. It generated a wave of suicides among young men (particularly university students) who identified with Werther's miseries. The job of management is to get people to focus on possibility, not potential disaster.

By the way, daydreaming in meetings is not necessarily a change-averse behaviour. Change can be made possible by recognising patterns through psychological dissociation and this is much more important today than ever before because the rules of modern life actively discourage, and at times even prohibit, what we call 'daydreaming.'

David Maister, the British management consultant, suggests questioning that focuses people on trying out new ideas:

- Why do you think we have this problem?
- What options do we have for doing things differently?
- What advantages do you foresee for the different options?
- How do you think the relevant players would react if we did that?
- How do you suggest we deal with the following adverse consequences of such an action?
- Other people have encountered the following diffi-

culties when they tried that. What can we do to prevent such things occurring?

- What benefits might come if we tried the following approach?

Anybody trying to effect change may have the answers but he/she shouldn't offer the answers. Listen, listen, listen. Ask empathic elaboration questions:

- 'Tell me more about...?'
- 'What's behind that?'
- 'Gosh, that must feel...'

The language of resistance to change is one key element groups need to address. The body language of change is also worth scrutiny. In my experience, when groups get to the physical behaviours, the first to surface is always the same: folded arms as an indicator of obduracy.

On this one, a word of caution is appropriate. It appears in all body language books and in most body language courses, as an infallible giveaway: when listeners fold their arms, they don't accept what you're saying to them. It ain't necessarily so, as the world-famous trial lawyer, Gerry Spence, who successfully defended Imelda Markos, found in an earlier trial. Just before this particular judicial outing, Spence attended a training course designed to help him read the body language of the members of any jury. As he argued the case for his client, his eyes scanned the jury box and delivered bad news. One big dungareed redneck at the back had his arms folded. Warning signs flashed in Spence's head and he went into overdrive to persuade that particular juror of the rightness of his cause. No use. The juror continued to keep his arms folded, right up to the moment the jury retired. Spence sat slumped, convinced this man would drag the rest of the jurors over to his negative view.

When the jury returned with their verdict, Gerry Spence

was floored to find their verdict favoured his client. He quickly congratulated him, bowed to the judge, and left the chamber in order to head off at the pass the man in the dungarees, who turned out to be quite agreeable to being asked questions about his behaviour. (Such questions can't be asked of jurors in Ireland.) No, he had not tried to sway the jury against Spence's client. He had, from the outset, been on the man's side. No, he had not hated the way Spence went about his business.

'You done good,' he told the attorney.

Spence pointed out that the juror had, throughout the trial, kept his arms folded, and shared with him the 'science' suggesting that his posture indicated hostility to the arguments being presented. The man's eyebrows rose and he looked pityingly at the lawyer.

'I got a big belly,' he pointed out. 'And a man's gotta put his arms someplace.'

It was as simple and insignificant as that. It is dangerous to attribute all-pervasive meaning to individual physical behaviour. Amateurs at lie-detection, for example, believe that putting a hand over the mouth is always proof that a man is lying. The man in my life, who is bluntly truthful in all situations, constantly puts his hand over his mouth at crucial points in a conversation. I don't know why. Not only does he not know why, he doesn't believe he does it. But it does not mean he's moving into falsehood territory.

Groups addressing behaviours indicative of reluctance to embrace change do, however, if pushed, frequently identify examples that are absolutely valid.

One of those behaviours is 'dead-catting' where someone resistant to change brings with them every day a metaphorical dead cat – an emerging problem – and presents it to the person trying to drive change. The response should always be: don't bring me your problems, solve them.

It's vital to remember that people are amazingly good at coping with positive change. Hand someone – particularly an 'early adopter', new technology, like an iPod, an iPhone or an iPad – and watch them teach themselves how to use it and serve as ambassadors for the product.

When we criticise someone as resistant to change, it is always negative change they object to. Nobody's happy to lose their job or to have to do the same job for less money in a situation in which they have less control. Control is the key. Any company or organisation introducing change should focus on getting its own staff to shape how the change will be managed. That's the key factor in eroding the instinct to look back, to continually ask why the change is necessary and to mourn for the past. Another key factor is the celebration of successful steps in the new direction. Too often, those in charge simply demand change but don't register the adjustments made by individuals or departments and the cumulative effect those adjustments deliver.

Threaded throughout any successful change process is communication. Constant, repetitive, two-way communication, always undertaken with the realisation neatly put by change management expert Bernard Burnes:

'As a rule of thumb, it should be recognised that, whilst people are often willing to believe the wildest rumour from unofficial sources, anything from management has to be stated at least six times in six different ways before people start giving it credence.'

You don't have to be flawed or phobic to be afraid of change. From our youngest days, we try to control our lives by reliance on the familiar – our favourite teddy or comfort blanket. As adults, we manage positive change amazingly well. Negative change, particularly if it affects our future, our finances or our sense of self, will always create fear. One simple question starts the process of turning that fear into fuel for the future:

'How can I make the best of this inevitable change?'

Fear of Rape

Rape has always been the crime of the violent victor, from the rape of the Sabine women depicted by Jacques-Louis David in the painting in the Louvre to the wholesale rape of women from geriatric to pre-teen by Russian soldiers in Germany after the collapse of the Third Reich.

Rape as a factor in urban life may be new, and, according to crime writer Colin Wilson, may result from a major change in the male's attitude to sex caused, believe it or not, by the invention of the typewriter in 1867. For the first time, he points out, relatively poor young ladies could now support themselves as typists.

'As the new class of working girls increased, a whole new type of "forbidden woman" came in to existence, like the vestal virgins in ancient Rome,' says Wilson. 'When James Boswell walked down Piccadilly or the Haymarket in 1750, he knew he could secure virtually any pretty girl, but if Boswell had walked through central London in 1890, he would have been surrounded by prim young ladies who would have been outraged if he had tried to pick them up. So the predatory male began to daydream of rape – the rape of prim, respectable girls.'

7

Fear of Public Speaking

Your mouth is dry and your palms are damp.

You woke up three times last night with an overwhelming sense of dread.

You have to make a speech. Or give a presentation.

And if you think you're alone with your terror, you couldn't be more wrong. Fear of public speaking comes at the top of the list of personal fears, way ahead of the dentist, despite the fact that so many people have to do it regularly as part of their job.

It's a transport problem, that fear. People who'd make you fall off a bar-stool with laughter can't transport their wit into the more pressured context of a boardroom. Friends whose emails are stuffed with interesting information get an attack of the waffles when they have to make a best-man speech. Co-workers who are brief and to the point on the phone go AWOL when speaking at a seminar.

Or, as a man named Howard Goshorn once said, 'The human brain is a wonderful thing. It operates from the moment you're born, until the moment you get up to make a speech.'

Good communicators often become bad public speakers because they listen to rotten advice. There's a lot of it about. Bad advice has a longer half-life than nuclear waste. It lives forever.

Take, for example, that mildewed old drivel that, when you stand up in front of an audience, you should:

- Tell them what you're going to tell them
- Tell it to them
- Tell them what you've told them

If the man in your life arrived home tonight and told you what he was going to talk about for the night, then talked at you, and ended up by summarising what he'd told you, you'd hit him with a brick or get him medical help. Nobody does that in real life, one-to-one, yet someone, back in the middle of the last century, decided people should always do it when they stand up in front of an audience. In other words: once enough individuals are unfortunate to get together in an audience, they can be treated like passive morons. Not only is this outrageously disrespectful to every individual present, it's totally dated.

Television changed the way people listen. Not for the better, but then television changed nothing for the better. It shortened the international attention span. But it also sharpened audiences' expectations. Audiences don't want big long context-setting introductions. They want speakers to be interesting, quickly.

Another piece of truly rotten advice is that oft-quoted bit of research alleging that 70 per cent of what an audience remembers after a presentation or a speech relates to the tone of the speaker's voice, their body language and their clothes.

What complete nonsense.

If 70 per cent of what the audience remembers is about voice, body language and clothes, it was one spectacularly lousy speech: they were so bored, they started to concentrate on the speaker's jacket, for God's sake. Put it another way. If you've been involved in an office Lotto syndicate and one of your colleagues arrives to tell you this week's ticket won and that you're a million Euro richer, the chances are kind of small that you'll make a mental note of the vocal tone, body language and wardrobe of the bearer of good news.

A great speech or presentation never starts with getting voice lessons or rehearsing gestures in front of a mirror.

A great speech or presentation starts with the audience. No, don't miss the importance of that.

A great speech or presentation starts with the audience.

Most public speakers start with themselves. With what they want to 'get across'. With the 'messages' they want to deliver. I may do violence to the next Head of Corporate Communications who sends their boss to me with a plea that I fix him or her because they get totally paralysed at the prospect of making a speech or a presentation, when 'we give them a complete PowerPoint with all the messageing in it'.

It's so wrong on so many fronts. First of all, the arrogance of starting with the determination to deliver messages, rather than the hope of creating a new understanding, is simply wrong in human terms. The second error is to hand a presenter a ready-made PowerPoint. Of course they're going to freeze. They didn't originate it. It isn't their ideas, their language, their references. Before you take pen or keyboard in hand, the first step is to sit down and work out who your audience is. Because a point that will make perfect sense to a thirty-two-year old mother of two, who owns an SUV and a Labrador, will not make perfect sense to a sixty-six-year old widower facing retirement. Write down a description of someone who represents the wider group you want to reach. Age. Gender. Location. Then add two additional bits of information:

- What they know – right now – about your topic
- What they feel – right now – about your topic

The next step is crucial. Write down what you want them to know and feel about your topic after you've finished. If you want them to make a decision or do something differently after your presentation, write that down, too.

Once you know who you're talking to and what you want to achieve, it's relatively simple to assemble a talk that will deliver that outcome.

You need a gateway point. A gateway point opens the door to the attention of your audience. Pick the single most interesting thing you want them to remember and put it at the top. Don't do lengthy introductions or settings-in-context. Cut to the chase. Grab them by the short and curlies.

Oh, and at this stage of your preparation, you shouldn't be sitting at a keyboard. Prepare for the spoken word in the spoken word. Walk around the room, making your points out loud. You'll often find that you don't like what you hear yourself saying. Contrariwise, you'll often love what you hear yourself saying. Write down what you like and keep talking until what you don't like fixes itself.

When you have worked out the key things you want re-membered, work out the best sequence for them, so they link logically one to another. Failure to have that logic, those seamless links, is where you put yourself in danger of drying up: O God, I don't know what comes next. A good present-ation has an organic shape to it. Like a tree. The speaker can illustrate a particular point (like the branch of a tree) but the central theme is always clear (like the trunk of the tree.)

It's only at this stage that a good public speaker considers using technology. Sadly, thousands of bad public speakers every day start to prepare by clicking on the PowerPoint icon on their computer. Public speaking would be immeasurably improved, worldwide, if a virus ate that icon and the program it goes with. PowerPoint is that paradoxical thing: an improvement that makes things worse. Some American corporations are now banning its use, because they find it interferes with the ability of their younger employees to do critical sequential thinking. Bluntly, they get hooked on bullet-points.

Bullet-points are new to human communication. They don't have a magical success story, reaching back into pre-history, like stories and pictures do. Every race in every country at every time since humanity started has relied on stories as a way of understanding the world around them, because stories are interesting, understandable and memorable: the three key qualifications for good communi-cation. We tell children fairy stories. We amuse pals with stories of disasters and gaffes. When it comes to public speaking, stories are an essential way to make the conceptual understandable.

For example, if a speaker says: 'Social outlets for otherwise anti-social tendencies are societally valuable,' we may be impressed, but we haven't gained understanding. If, on the other hand, the speaker puts the concept into a story, everybody understands the concept: 'My ten-year-old son plays soccer three times a week. That gives him a chance to work off all the energy that – if it was stored up inside him – might have him throwing stones or scribbling graffiti on the wall down the road.'

Pictures are important, too. If a speaker describes something so vividly that everybody in the audience gets a mental picture, it improves the chances that they will remember the picture and the point it makes, because synapses spark in their brain because of the effort to visualise.

Which brings us to the problems posed by PowerPoint. A PowerPoint picture is not worth a thousand words – because the audience gets it handed to them. They don't have to work to create it in their own heads, and so are less likely to remember it.

An even worse problem with PowerPoint is where it's used by speakers as a prompt for themselves. Prompts are necessary – and we'll come to the best method in a moment – but inflicting your reminders on an audience as if it served their needs, when it clearly doesn't, is counter-productive. The moment a PowerPoint presentation starts, the alpha waves in the brains of the audience flatten, as they decide, 'OK, this doesn't require any active involvement from me. Passivity rules.'

Cards are inarguably the best prompt method. Not a million tiny cards. A few sizeable cards. Carrying trigger words, not full sentences, written with a thick black felt-tip pen, twice the size of the speaker's normal handwriting, because the speaker will be under pressure and the words must leap off the cards at a glance.

Then it's rehearsal, to the point where the sequence and the illustrations are familiar, but not to the point where it's learned off by heart.

Still nervous? Good. You should be.

Fear of PowerPoint: Nextslideitis

Fear of PowerPoint is not only justified, it is meritorious. PowerPoint is a corporate reflex so embedded in many companies that to make a presentation without PowerPoint is to seem unprepared. This, despite the fact that nobody pays any real attention to the presentation when it's being made, because they'll get the printout later.

I have clients I suspect of opening their PCs to do a PowerPoint response to domestic questions like: 'Will you put out the wheelie bin?' Without it, they're not capable of thought. With it, they can render everybody else incapable of thought.

Author David Brooks likens victimhood by PowerPoint to the fate of the low-level 'grunts' in an army.

'They will march straight into the hail of bullet-points,' he writes. 'They will endure hour upon hour of jargonics, the unique sales-conference language, receiving valuable advice on how they can prioritise their cost-effective operational performance and increase network function-ality while magnifying their brand power through strategic B-to-B partnering in ways that will leverage their compet-itive-advantage matrixes without sacrificing any of their core-competency components or their multiple-vendor, mission-critical supply-chain service-provider solution resources. The slides flow by on the screen like one of those May Day Soviet missile parades, so that after forty-five minutes of Leadership, Quality, Change, and Excellence, the speaker could have his girlfriend's sex diary up on the screen and nobody would even notice.'

Fear of Making a Gaffe

You don't know which knife to use, or how to address someone famous or how to describe someone from a different ethnic group. The fear of making a social gaffe goes back to the Middle Ages when courtiers competed with one another about who would display the most exquisite, nuanced and civilised behaviour. More recently, novelist Nancy Mitford terrified a generation of the new middle class by categorising behaviours into U and non-U. Unacceptable behaviours fell under the non-U category heading and included saying 'Pleased to meet you,' when introduced to someone, instead of 'How do you do?'

Many people, when they're fearful of making a gaffe, fail to do the obvious: ask. If, for example, you're at a formal dinner and you have no clue how or with which implement to eat what's put in front of you, the simplest and most effective action is to tell the person next to you that you haven't a clue and ask for their help. People love to be asked for help.

If you have to introduce or address someone, you can check in either the *IPA Yearbook and Diary* or *This Business of Writing*, or telephone their office and ask their assistant for help. That's also the route to go when you can't pronounce a name or don't know how to describe someone. For example, some people get worried about describing someone as a Jew, and go for Jewish as being somehow warmer: but the first is correct. The rule is simple: call people what they call themselves, and find out what it is. Members of the travelling community, for instance, call themselves travellers. Not itinerants.

Speaking in public gives you the opportunity to put a new idea in someone's head. To make a group see the world in a different way. To give someone in your audience an insight that may change their life.

That's important. If you're the vehicle for someone else's

breakthrough, it's important that you are properly tense before you start. Nerves are good. Actors believe that the day they stand in the wings and are not nervous is the day they've burned out: they need that adrenalin-rush of pure terror to do a good job.

Finally, look at your audience. Not at the EXIT sign. Within minutes, one of them will nod in response to a point you've made. Or smile at you. When that happens, it is the beginning of a relationship with all of them. Trust them. Because if you do, they will trust you right back – and your fear will evaporate.

8

Fear of Boredom

You may not have regarded boredom as anything but a minor irritant, but it's a lot more than that. Research shows that if you are bored at work, not only does your IQ seem to get lower, but you are three to five times more likely to develop cardiovascular disease. That's just one of the disorders to which boredom seems to make people vulnerable, and which make it more likely that a bored person will make mistakes. Or worse.

British writer J.B. Priestley maintained that boredom plays a part in people going to war. In the 1930s, many of his peers were part of the pacifist movement, which never really caught on with the general public, largely, he believed, because of a boredom leading to 'the widespread desire for some grand piece of excitement, for fiery speeches and flag-waving, for special editions, troop trains, casualty lists.'

Now, in the aftermath of *Bowling for Columbine* and other accounts of shocking violence perpetrated by bored teenagers, here's a quotation from a twelve-year-old. Bend your mind to predict how this little charmer will turn out, when he grows up.

'Often I'd like to be able to blow the heads off passersby,' he recorded in his diary. 'I am bored, I am bored, I am bored.'

Gustave Flaubert – for that was the name of the pre-teen – became one of France's greatest novelists. He always had a fantasy that travel would erase his boredom, but was, as an adult, so dissatisfied with the travel he did that he wrote about that, too, in resentful terms:

We saw stars
And waves; we saw sand too
And, despite many crises and unforeseen disasters,
We were often bored, just as we are here.

Cheery soul, wasn't he? You have to be glad he was born before the motor car was developed. He'd have done iambic pentameter versions of 'Are we there yet?'

Martin Heidegger once defined boredom as 'the hot breath of nothingness on our necks'. In the late nineteenth and early twentieth century, the hot breath of nothingness created by a repetitive task and added to the heat of their surroundings made the cigar-making factories in Florida's Key West and Tampa singularly difficult places in which to work, until management showed some imagination and employed extra staff members to read to the workforce.

Those who fulfilled the role of lector or 'reader' tended to be articulate, well-informed and possessed of enough lung power to be heard by large numbers of cigar makers. (They would not, of course, have had such lung power, had they been consumers of the factory's product, but we'll gloss over that.) They read novels aloud. They read poetry. They read newspapers. All in an attempt to stave off boredom. They undoubtedly lightened the load of the mindless monotony of a cigar-maker's daily work. But they did much more than that. They became a running tutorial, ensuring that their listeners became 'well-informed and surprisingly well read', in the words of American novelist John Dos Passos. When he spent time in Key West, his favourite companions were the expatriate Cuban cigar-rollers, and he spent time in the factories in order to see the lectors in action and to observe which material the workers preferred. He reported that they 'listened with avidity not only to the socialist newspapers, but to the nineteenth-century Spanish novelists and to translations of Dostoevsky and Tolstoy.'

It's safe to assume that not many of the books the lectors read aloud figured in a list developed through a survey conducted by Columbia University in 1950, in which they asked booksellers, librarians and teachers to pick out the most boring classics of all time. *The Pilgrim's Progress* headed the list, followed by *Moby Dick*, *Paradise Lost*, *The Faerie Queen* and Boswell's *Life of Johnson*. Even if they did, in another exemplification of an improvement that makes things worse, piped music became available following the discovery of electricity and the development of technology to record and transmit. In consequence, the ongoing tutorials not only failed to catch on elsewhere but died out in the cigar factories.

As the early cigar-factory managers realised, boredom is inextricably bound up with repetitive tasks that don't challenge the worker. But boredom surfaces during leisure time, too, and affects more than children. A phenomenon called 'Sunday boredom' has popped up in recent research. It's the kind that's experienced only on Sundays and bank holidays. People who really enjoy their day job sometimes find that holidays constitute a nightmare of sunny nothingness rendered tolerable only by the mobile phone in their fist and Internet capability in their hotel.

Sunday boredom and holiday boredom (see Chapter 5), felt by people who would prefer to be at work, are some of the things that have contributed to a school of thought, nowadays, suggesting that our fear of boredom is worse than the boredom itself. It swallows us, when we are not working, into lives of shapeless addiction to iPhones, iPads, YouTube and reruns of *The West Wing* or, if we are teenagers, texting, Facebook and reruns of *Entourage*.

'If you think of boredom as the prelude to creativity, and loneliness as the prelude to engagement of the imagination, then they are good things,' says Dr Edward Hallowell, a cognitive expert and author of the book *CrazyBusy*. 'They are doorways to something better, as opposed to something to be abhorred and eradicated immediately.'

Fear of Temptation

Oscar Wilde said he could resist anything except temptation. And the Catholic Church used to hand out the best advice about temptation. The Church used to tell people to avoid what it called 'occasions of sin'. In other words, if you're likely to be tempted to have extra-marital sex, cruising a red light district is a bad idea. If you're addicted to gambling, it's not a bad idea to steer clear of the bookie's shop.

A professor of nutritional science at Cornell recently did a simple experiment related to the temptation issue. Brian Wansink put bowls holding toffees on the desks of office workers. These were pretty isolated office workers. Not many people passed their desks, so it was easy to work out who ate the toffees. Some of the bowls had clear glass lids. Some had opaque lids. What the researchers found was that the workers who could see the sweets all the time, through the clear glass lids, were 71 per cent more likely to scoff them than were the workers whose bowls had lids it was impossible to see through. The Professor summed up the lesson of his little test by pointing out that the bowls with clear glass lids provided temptation every five minutes.

'It means having to say no twelve times the first hour, twelve times the second hour and so on. Eventually, some of those nos turn into yeses.'

If you know you have a constant temptation, whether that temptation takes the form of food, drinks, alcohol, anti-social behaviour, bitching or worrying, you stand a better chance of resisting it if you don't hang around in places where you can see it, hear it, smell it or talk to it.

Dr Richard Ralley, a British psychology lecturer, has begun a large-scale study of boredom, which he considers a neglected area. Motivated in part by the spectacle of parents tying themselves in knots trying to keep their children entertained during the summer holidays with camps of every possible sort, from horses to yoga, he advises: 'Boredom is something, it's not just switching off. It can be useful. When there's nothing rewarding going on we conserve energy, so that when we want to re-engage we can.'

9

Fear of Hospitals

The system operating in 1847 was simple and random. If a patient arrived on the first day of the week, they went to Division One in the Allgemaine Krankenhous, part of the vast hospital built by Emperor Joseph II in Vienna in his mother's honour. Its buildings included the largest lying-in hospital in the world, divided into two divisions: Division One run by physicians, the other by midwives. The allocation of parents made sense to the staff. It made no sense to the patients, who made no secret of their reaction when they were told to which Division they were headed.

'That they were afraid of the First Division there was abundant evidence,' an obstetrician wrote. 'Many heart-rending scenes occurred when patients found out that they had entered the First Division by mistake. They knelt down, wrung their hands and begged that they might be discharged.'

If they ended up in a bed in Division One, the same obstetrician noted, and even if they had the fever and swelling indicative of severe infection, mothers would not give up.

'They would protest that they were really quite well, in order to avoid medical treatment, for they believed that the doctor's interference was always the precursor of death.'

The man writing down what he was seeing every day was a clever twenty-eight year old Viennese obstetrician named Ignaz Semmelweis. He was an obsessive data-gatherer who loved statistics as much as human stories. The statistics of his hospital worried him. Every year, some 3000 mothers were delivered of their babies there. At least 20 per cent of them – 600 per year – died of puerperal or childbed fever. Of course, this was the nineteenth century, and of course outbreaks of childbed fever happened in maternity hospitals throughout Europe. But the apparent inevitability of the disease and the mortality rate of the women attending the hospital had to be weighed against the fact that only 1 per cent of mothers having home births in Vienna during those years died.

But there were other, even more troubling comparisons to be made within the hospital itself. The mothers-to-be who regarded themselves as doomed when they were sent to Division One and who begged to go to the division they regarded as immeasurably safer had only anecdotal evidence to support them. They weren't privy to the hospital's statistics. But Semmelweis was, and it bothered him that the year before he had taken up employment in Vienna's General Hospital, while 459 women had died in the Division One, only a quarter of that number, 105, had died in Division Two.

With hindsight, it seems screamingly obvious that something bad was happening in Division One that definitely wasn't happening in Division Two and that the only thing necessary to save on average 500 lives a year was to compare and contrast.

It didn't happen. At the time, the 'miasma' theory of infection was widely held. Somehow or other, this theory proposed, a miasma or unseen mist of bad stuff came from somewhere which infected and killed patients. The evidence is still to be seen in Dublin's Rotunda Hospital where, around the same time as Semmelweis was working in Vienna, concern was surfacing about the mortality rate due to puerperal fever.

The obstetricians came up with a cunning plan to vent the miasma they knew was causing it. They would put wrought-iron circular grids in the floor and semi-circular versions atop the walls of the corridors, thereby improving the circulation of air and the dispersal of malign miasma. In went the grids. Down came the mortality rate. Up went the reputations of the Master and his pals. Nobody noticed that around the same time, the midwives in the hospital had come together and decided that it wasn't pleasant for any woman to have to give birth on a bed of hay covered in blood from a previous birth, as was the practice at the time. They brought in fresh hay each time. Which of course removed an obvious infection-carrier. It was the action of the midwives (taken, it must be said, in the interests of patient comfort rather than safety) that caused the death rate to drop. The midwives went to their graves in forgotten anonymity, which is a bit tough, given that they had saved so many women from an agonising death which orphaned their babies, in cases where the babies survived.

Meanwhile, in Vienna, Semmelweis, examining the shockingly different outcomes in the midwives' division as contrasted with the obstetricians' division, had followed Sherlock Holmes's dictum that 'Once you eliminate the impossible, whatever remains, no matter how improbable, must be the truth,' and worked out that the doctors themselves were carrying the disease between patients. But if that was the case, why weren't the midwives doing the same? For starters, because they were much less interventive than the consultants, much less likely to insert their hands into the patient than were the men.

However, one additional factor differentiated the consultants from the midwives. Because the hospital had such a shocking level of puerperal fever, it was the Mecca for anybody who wanted to study the disease, and the consultants within the Allgemeine Krankenhaus did autopsies on the constantly-available dead bodies. They then visited and examined newly-admitted patients, bringing the infection with them on their unwashed hands to create a perfect continuum of disaster.

Semmelweis insisted that every doctor and nurse scrub with a nail brush and chlorine between patients. The death rate immediately dropped like a stone. It went right down to 1 per cent. Evidence? Yes. Proof? Incontrovertible. Except that many of his colleagues found unacceptable the idea that they had been murderers and would continue to kill, as long as they did not observe his nit-picky requirements. Understandably, perhaps, they retreated from self-inculpation and reasserted their faith in the miasma theory of infection, helped by Semmelweis's failure to publish an explanation of his theory or undertake a scientific experiment, using animals, to prove it. He seemed to think that his colleagues were insulting him by asking for proof and he had no understanding of how one human being persuades another to change a long-standing behaviour pattern.

'You, Herr Professor, have been a partner in this massacre,' he wrote to one University of Vienna obstetrician who didn't buy the idea that bowls of chlorine solution could save lives. To another colleague he wrote, 'Should you, Herr Hofrath, without having disproved my doctrine, continue to teach your pupils [against it], I declare before God and the world that you are a murderer and the *History of Childbed Fever* would not be unjust to you if it memorialised you as a medical Nero.'

Nor did he confine himself to infuriating people in print. He would stand beside the chlorine bowls and give out stink to anyone who forgot to use them. He was fired, taking his passion and his intemperate methods of communication to another hospital, where he began to behave strangely. Eventually even his wife acknowledged that he had lost his reason and he was consigned to a lunatic asylum where he quickly died, undoubtedly from the beatings administered by asylum staff as a way of subduing him.

The Semmelweis tragedy meant that the truth very definitely did not set the pregnant women of Vienna free. They continued to die in their thousands. It was a long, long time before Lister came up with the same conclusion but presented it with clear evidence and a respectful plea for antisepsis in surgery in the British medical journal *The Lancet*.

If the fear, in maternity hospitals, was of infection and death, the fear in military hospitals, as Florence Nightingale found out during the Boer War, lay elsewhere. She insisted on placing a screen around the bed of a man who was to undergo amputation of a limb, because, she pointed out, the fear engendered in a soldier by watching someone experiencing such surgery tended to militate against his chances of surviving such surgery himself.

When British soldiers reduced to 'miserable skeletons devoured by lice' arrived at her hospital in Scutari, suffering from wounds, frostbite, fever and dysentery, Nightingale made sure they were washed, given clean beds, and fed good food. She fired nurses found to be drunk on the ward.

'It may seem a strange principle to enunciate as the very first requirement in a hospital that it should do the sick no harm,' she later observed in a book about nursing. 'It is quite necessary, nevertheless, to lay down such a principle, because the actual mortality in hospitals, especially in those of large cities, is very much higher than any calculation founded on the mortality of the same class of diseases among patients treated out of hospital would lead us to expect. It is now a well-known rule: keep no patient in hospital a day longer than is absolutely necessary…And even this may be days too long. The patient may have to recover not only from illness or injury but from hospital.'

Then, as now, people going into hospital are afraid on two fronts. They're afraid of being treated badly, although not in a medical sense, and they're afraid of developing an iatrogenic infection. The management guru Peter Drucker, once published research showing that the single most important need of a patient is for 'assurance.' Back in the mid-nineteenth century, Florence Nightingale addressed precisely the same issue.

'Apprehension, uncertainty, waiting and fear of surprise, do a patient more harm than any exertion,' she wrote. 'Always tell a patient, and tell him beforehand, when you are going out and when you will be back, whether it is for a day, an hour or ten minutes.'

The other issue is infection.

Nightingale regarded hospital infection as preventable, and unforgiveable when it occurred.

Today, two million people in the United States contract dangerous infections every year during their stay in one of the nation's hospitals.

'As many as 90,000 people die every year from these infections,' TV commentator Lou Dobbs points out. 'This is a staggering number: Healthcare-associated infections kill more than two hundred people a day.'

According to Dr Atul Gawande, who has written extensively on improvements in healthcare, the hardest part of any infection-control team's job is not coping with the variety of contagions they encounter, the speed at which they occur, or the panic that sometimes occurs among patients and staff. Instead, their greatest difficulty is getting clinicians like Gawande to do the one thing that consistently halts the spread of infections: wash their hands.

'Our hospital's statistics show what studies everywhere else have shown – that we doctors and nurses wash our hands one-third to one-half as often as we are supposed to. Having shaken hands with a sniffling patient, pulled a sticky dressing off someone's wound, pressed a stethoscope against a sweating chest, most of us do little more than wipe our hands on our white coats and move on – to see the next patients, to scribble a note in the chart, to grab some lunch.'

Atul Gawande ruefully looks back a century and a half to the unfortunate Ignaz Semmelweis, driven out of his mind by the futility of his – similar – struggles to get medical staff to realise that by failing to wash their hands before examining patients, they were causing some of those patients to die in a plague created by doctors.

'140 years of doctors' plagues later, however, you have to wonder whether what's needed to stop them is precisely a lunatic,' Gawande says.

Given that it has been proven that the primary vector for the transmission of the SARS virus is the hands of healthcare workers, he adds, anything short of a Semmelweis-like obsession with hand-washing has begun to seem inadequate.

'We always hope for the easy fix: the one simple change that will erase a problem in a stroke. But few things in life work this way. Instead, success requires making a hundred small steps go right – one after the other, no slipups, no goofs, everyone pitching in. We are used to thinking of doctoring as a solitary, intellectual task. But making medicine go right is less often like making a difficult diagnosis than like making sure everyone washes their hands. It is unsettling to find how little it takes to defeat success in medicine.

'Why, after 140 years, the meticulousness of the operating room has not spread beyond its double doors is a mystery. But the people who are most careful in the surgical theatre are frequently the very ones who are least careful on the hospital ward. I know because I have realised I am one of them. I generally try to be as scrupulous about washing my hands when I am outside the operating room as I am inside. And I do pretty well, if I say so myself. But then I blow it. It happens almost every day. I walk into a patient's hospital room, and I'm thinking about what I have to tell him concerning his operation, or about his family, who might be standing there looking worried, or about the funny little joke a resident had just told me, and I completely forget about getting a squirt of that gel onto my palms. Sometimes I do remember, but before I can find the dispenser, the patient puts his hand out in greeting and I think it too strange not to go ahead and take it. On occasion I even think, "Screw it – I'm late, I have to get a move on, and what difference does it really make what I do this one time?"'

Gwande's frankness about his own instincts is borne out, again and again, by the statistics. A study of a ward of newborn babies in a hospital in Chicago showed that while nurses followed hand-washing guidelines about half the time; doctors in the ward followed the guidelines half as frequently as that.

The problem is reliance on antibiotics rather than on hygiene and the failure to realise that a simple, relatively unsophisticated and cheap measure – washing hands – can be so effective.

Over-reliance on myth is another problem. Myth like the value of the white coat some doctors wear.

'But a white coat might be positively bad for our health as patients, precisely because the white appearance lulls us into believing it is cleaner than it might really be,' writes British doctor and TV presenter Raj Persaud. 'The startling recent finding is that white coats are a reservoir of extremely virulent germs. They have been found to be commonly contaminated with the antibiotic-resistant bacterium *Staphylococcus aureus* – the bug that is found in abscesses and boils – and *Pseudomonas aeruginosa* – a germ commonly found in infected urine. So alarmed were infection-control specialists by the bugs they could grow from white coats, that some hospitals, like the James Paget Trust in Norfolk, have now discontinued white coats for doctors.'

Now let's go back to the theme of this chapter: fear of going to hospital. It's a justified fear. But, as patients and visitors, we can do something about it. The first thing we can do is not torment our GP for antibiotics. Antibiotics are damn all use for infections like the common cold, but over-use of antibiotics is causing the morphing of bacteria into antibiotic-resistant bugs that could kill. According to Dr Edmond Smyth, President of the Irish Society of Clinical Microbiologists, bacteria have evolved more in the last sixty years (since the introduction of antibiotics) than they did in all the millennia up to then. The bugs, in short, are infinitely adaptable, and over-use of antibiotics triggers their adaptation into antibiotic resistant forms.

The second thing we can do, as visitors, is to use the sanitising gel that's at the entrances to all hospitals.

The third is the most difficult. It's about protecting ourselves from other people. Including medical professionals who – as Atul Gawande admits – now and again fail to follow the rules they know to be important. If you're a patient or a patient's relative and you see a medic about to begin an examination which involves touching the patient without first washing their hands, then you need to ask politely that they do so.

They won't like you for telling them this. Bluntly, however, this is your choice: being popular or being safe. You pick.

The fear of having to go to hospital has a long history and much evidence to support it. Just remember, if you face the prospect of hospitalisation, that the more preparation you do and the more questions you ask in advance of packing your bag, the fewer surprises will happen to you when you become a patient. Remember also that every hospital has a complaints procedure, so if anything unpleasant happens to you while you're there, that need not be the end of it. Unlike the unfortunate mothers-to-be who were reluctantly admitted to Division One of the Allgemaine Krankenhous, you have choices and rights and a variety of ways to express both.

Fear of Drink

In past centuries, it was safer to drink beer than to drink water. But then, beer and wine were not as strong as they are today.

Even so, spirits, wine and beer were used for the same reasons we use them today: to raise courage, dull pain and reduce inhibition. They also had the same disastrous outcomes. It's recorded, for example, that in Manchester in 1635, a man who had been drinking heavily was eventually refused another pint by the barmaid. He promptly 'swore he would drink ten dozens that night' and left for another alehouse 'far into the night', only to fall into a pit and drown. Around the same time, a man in Derby, after a night's drinking, fell into a ditch where he snored so loudly that someone took him for a rabid dog and shot him dead.

Sébastien Mercier's portrait of what he observed in Paris around the same time goes along similar lines. 'In vain the semi-blind leads the blind, each step is perilous, the ditch waits for them both, or rather the wheels,' he wrote.

Then came the gin craze, which devastated English cities. Temperance movements began in modern times as people began to realise just how much damage alcohol does. In 1915, David Lloyd George, then Chancellor of the Exchequer and a well-known supporter of the Temperance movement, claimed that alcohol was causing 'more damage in the war than all the submarines put together'.

Few lives are improved by alcohol, and if you're afraid of it, possibly because you've seen, up close and familial, the damage it can do, then steer clear of it. Being teetotal isn't a crime.

10

Fear of Flying: Aerophobia

'Now is when the dangerous part of your journey begins,' the Southwest Airlines pilot says. 'Please be careful driving home.'

Disembarking passengers smile ruefully at each other. Of course, they know rationally that airline travel is a thousand times safer than driving, but what's rational got to do with it? It has been estimated that you're roughly seven times more at risk of death in a car than in a plane, but fear of flying is a constant human terror, whereas fear of driving is rare.

Since the beginning, flying has terrified passengers. Comedian P.J. Gallegher was so terrified of flying that he actually studied for and won a private pilot's licence. Paradoxically, it seemed the best way of coping with the terror. It worked, too. But before we look at this and other ways of coping with this disabling terror, it's important to make the point that our capacity to analyse risk is somewhere between bad and appalling. So we hugely overestimate the danger of flying and ridiculously underestimate the dangers of activities in which we engage on a daily basis, including driving, cycling, drinking, going without sleep, climbing the stairs, using a ladder and smoking.

Michael Jackson was afraid of flying, but then Michael Jackson was afraid of everything except Disneyland. Woody Allen probably has aerophobia too, but then he's afraid of everything other than Manhattan. (So far, he's confessed to fear of insects, sunshine, dogs, deer, bright colours, crowds, heights, children – and let's have no smart cracks down the back, please – and small rooms.) Cher, Jennifer Aniston and Whoopi Goldberg all have aerophobia. At least they can own or charter their own planes, so they don't have to cope with the toddler in the next seat who clicks the seat-belt mechanism 1,345,642 times during the flight.

Flying gets safer with every passing year, but humans became imprinted, early, with the twin notions of danger and glamour. The danger came from the early accidents. Just eight years after the Wright Brothers made their first brief flight a young man named Calbraith Pery Rodgers decided to compete for a prize offered by Randolph Hearst, the newspaperman, for the first person to cross the USA from coast to coast by flight and return within thirty days. Rodgers had all of ninety minutes of flying instruction under his belt and sixty flying hours. On the journey, he experienced almost every danger other than UFOs, but, having started from Sheepshead Bay, New York on 17 September, 1911, in a plane that had no brakes, so that it had to be held on the ground by volunteers until he gave a signal to free it, he reached Pasadena. Then it was time for the return journey. He didn't make it within the thirty days but he did create a record.

Sadly, having done the nearly impossible, just a few months later he borrowed a plane for a short spin over Long Beach. The little plane encountered a flock of seagulls and ended up in the sea about three hundred yards from where Rodgers had started his epic westward journey. His neck was broken and he died within days; the first but by no means the last pilot to have his plane downed by a bird strike.

As passenger air travel began to become a reality, those running the embryonic airlines realised that they had to cope with the fear factor. They did it in a number of ways. They dressed pilots and co-pilots in quasi-military garb, sending the message of authority and of someone being in charge. The cabin staff – female – were selected for their looks and their capacity to comfort, feed and distract the anxious.

Yet, every now and then, an horrendous crash would happen that would reinforce fear of flying in those who already suffered from it. The photographs of the wreckage would take over the front pages of newspapers, together with the names of any famous person who happened to be on board. At the same time, automobile traffic was increasing, together with its enormous death rates, but – with notable exceptions – car crashes kill two or three people at a time, whereas a single plane crash could result in the loss of hundreds of lives.

Even when plane crashes brought about no fatalities, they could be frightening. One teacher with a fairly pronounced fear of flying was due to fly from Dublin Airport to Liverpool to take up a teaching post there in September 1956. He was feeling iffy enough about the flight before his taxi turned a corner on the Swords Road and he found himself facing a plane straddling the road, just across from the airport. It was a flight from Lourdes that had come down a bit short of the runway. The teacher considered his position while the taxi was diverted around the tail end of the plane but decided to rely on the law of averages and go for it.

For that teacher, and a generation of sports fans, the definitive air crash horror happened on 6 February 1958. It snowed that day in Ireland. Unfortunately, it also snowed in Munich. On the runway in Munich-Riem airport, West Germany, was a BEA Airspeed Ambassador turbo prop, Flight 609. Almost half the passengers were footballers from the Manchester United football team, known as the 'Busby Babes,' because the manager of Man U at that time was Sir Matt Busby, who, incidentally, hated the 'Busby Babes' nickname as doing an injustice to young lads he saw as behaving in a way that was older than their years. Also on the plane were journalists and team supporters on their way back from the European Cup match in Belgrade, Yugoslavia, against Red Star Belgrade.

The plane refuelled in Munich and made two attempts to take off, but had problems with the port engine. It was on the third attempt that it foundered, slowed by slush on the runway. Ploughing through a fence and losing a wing when it hit a house, it burst into flames. Captain Thain, the pilot, and some of the footballers who had not been injured, mindful of the fact that those who had been knocked unconscious were in terrible danger because of fire and the potential of explosion, went back into the damaged plane and pulled survivors from the destroyed plane. Matt Busby was grievously injured, and Captain Thain underwent a decade of public opprobrium before he was cleared of culpability. New safety regulations were introduced to cope with the dangers of snow, slush and ice as a result of the Munich air disaster.

The crash had a huge impact on sports-mad teenagers in Ireland at the time, who can to this day reel off the names of the survivors (twenty-one) and casualties (twenty-three) alike.

'Harry Gregg, Billy Foulkes – goalkeeper for the six counties – and Bobby Charlton came out alive,' one man who is terrified of flying remembers. 'Bobby Charlton had minor injuries. Harry Gregg was really brave – he went back into the plane and got others out.'

One of the consequences was a changed view of where to sit in a plane. When sports fans talked about the crash, the word spread that the members of the Manchester United team who were saved were in the tail end of Flight 609. Others claimed that a seat over the wing was the safest position.

My friend, who had always been terrified of flying, encountered a pilot at a party a few months after Munich.

'If a plane is going to crash and you're a passenger, where's the safest place for you to be sitting?' he asked.

'If you were a pilot and you were going to crash, who would you save?' was the smiling response.

'The pilot?'

The other man nodded.

'So I should sit up at the front, as near the pilot as possible?'

A nod was his answer. The pilot involved must be forgiven for misleading his interlocutor, but the fact is that the nearer you are to the back in a plane, in the event of a crash, the better. Statistically. Passengers seated towards the rear of the aircraft are 40 per cent more likely to survive than those seated in the first few rows. That's the conclusion of a *Popular Mechanics* study of every commercial air crash in the USA since 1971. The study revealed no steady pattern. In some crashes, everybody at the back died: in others, everybody at the front. But when you even it out, the advantage seems to lie with sitting as far away from the pilot as you can get.

Before you take too much comfort from that finding, it should be admitted that it was contradicted, in summer 2011, by a study done by the University of Greenwich, commissioned by Britain's Civil Aviation Authority, which checked out accounts given by 2000 survivors of more than a hundred aviation accidents throughout the world. In these crashes, it seemed that passengers at the front of the plane had a 65 per cent chance of escape, while those at the rear had a 10 per cent lower chance of getting out.

This study also found what should, in retrospect, have been bleedin' obvious: your chances of getting out of a plane in the event of a disaster are greatly improved if you're close to an emergency exit. Whether the seat is on the aisle or not doesn't make much difference, although an aisle seat is marginally safer.

Or you could look at it another way. If you're the sort of passenger who reads the safety leaflet, asks for a seat no more than five rows from an exit and checks out where all exits are long before you relax and look at one of the available movies, you're much more likely to survive a plane crash anyway. It's neither the seat nor the statistics that will save your life in a crash. It's you.

Not that we should knock the statistics, because, on this issue, they're pretty comforting.

First of all, the chances of your plane falling out of the sky or getting into an argument with a hill are quite small. The average passenger getting on to the average flight has a one in sixty million chance of being killed on that flight. The odds of getting killed in a car crash are closer to one in nine million.

Most people understand that air crashes are rare and

that flying is a safe form of transport, yet nonetheless are convinced that, in the event of their plane falling out of the sky, everybody on board will die. That is not the case. More than 95 per cent of people involved in air crashes survive.

'Contrary to public perception,' says the US National Transport Safety Board, 'the most likely outcome of an accident is that most of the occupants survived.'

Few passengers know this statistic. Does it matter? The answer is probably, 'Yes.' If you believe you can survive a plane crash, you might be less likely to freeze in position if the worst happens.

Freezing in position happens more often than you'd like to imagine. It's sometimes likened to what happens to baby chicks if the shadow of a hawk passes over them. They instantly develop what's called 'tonic immobility'. They turn into little chicken statues. Which may be helpful, because the hawk may not realise that those small yellow rocks down below are actually available fast food.

It's not quite the same in humans, although it looks identical. According to Ben Sherwood, a former Rhodes Scholar at Oxford who has studied survival traits, when human beings freeze in place, thereby endangering their own survival in a catastrophe, their immobility is caused by quite a different confluence of factors.

'As your frontal lobes process the sight of an aeroplane wing on fire,' Sherwood wrote in his seminal *Survivors' Club*, an examination of the traits and characteristics of people who don't die when others – faced with the same challenging circumstances – do, 'If you have no stored experience of a plane crash, your brain can't find a match and gets stuck in a loop of trying and failing to come up with the right response. Hence: immobility.'

It's not that the passengers who move fast and save their own lives don't panic. They do – but their particular panic impels them into action, whereas the same panic causes others to sit, locked into immobility. Significantly, the indications are that this immobility is *not* caused by failure to grasp the dire consequences of what's going on.

'On the contrary, [the immobile passenger] knows that if nothing is done, severe pain and even death will probably occur – but still he does nothing,' says Daniel Johnson, an aviation safety expert. It sounds like the accounts of people who have woken up in the middle of surgical operations because of a failure of the general anaesthetic but who are unable to do anything about the agony they're in.

The bottom line seems to be that if your brain locks up in response to an overload of unprecedented information, you're likely to wait for instructions and respond only to external leadership rather than get the hell out of the burning fuselage in the few seconds available to you. This may be complicated by the attitude you had before the flight. If you believe your chances of getting out alive from a plane crash are somewhere between slim and non-existent, you don't pay attention when the flight attendant goes through the safety palaver at the outset, you don't crane your neck to establish where the emergency exit nearest you is and you don't read the safety leaflet in the seat pocket in front of you. If your fatalism is complicated by terror, you may anaesthetise yourself with alcohol or knock yourself out with a sleeping pill or Dramamine. In the event of a crash, therefore, your capacity to cope is demonstrably reduced by lack of information complicated by being drunk, asleep or chemically restrained. That doesn't mean you shouldn't sleep on a flight. It just means being awake, alert and informed during the first three minutes of a flight and the last eight. That's the danger time. Eight out of ten air accidents happen during these periods.

The information necessary to survive an air crash has to be more than read. It has to be internalised. Research indicates that even when people have glanced around them to locate the emergency exit nearest them, that information doesn't necessarily lock itself into their short-term memory, so that in the unlikely event of a crash, with a plane filling with smoke, they may not be able to locate the exit they thought they had 'learned'. Survival experts say that instead of reading the newspaper or the menu at the beginning of a flight, you're better off to memorise precisely how many seat backs separate you from your nearest exit. If something goes wrong, you need to take intelligent action, quickly.

'Of course, this idea runs contrary to the entire experience of going to the airport and flying these days,' Ben Sherwood admits. 'Every step of the way, from ticketing to security to boarding, you're told exactly what to do and when to do it. Too many passengers carry that passive mentality into a crash.'

Passivity doesn't save lives on a troubled flight. The single most important survival factor is the capacity to respond quickly and calmly to the opportunity.

When Air France Flight 358 going into Toronto five years ago in gusting winds and heavy rains overshot the runway, plunged into a ravine and burst into flames, all 309 passengers got out alive. Not only did they get out alive, despite some of the exits being out of commission, they all did it within the requisite ninety seconds.'

If you climb on board a plane with pre-existing disadvantages, you need to work even harder at managing your own safety. The people who get first out of plane wrecks tend to be young, fit and male. Surprise, Surprise. The people least likely to get out are older, fatter women. But in one simulated evacuation, a passenger weighing more than four hundred pounds got out in less than two minutes.

The very fact that air travel is such a phenomenally safe form of transport may contribute to the learned helplessness of passengers. But the fact is that, in the event of an accident, the odds on your coming out alive are greatly enhanced if you take charge of your safety. Before you actually need to. (If you're female, don't wear tights or nylon knee socks. In the event of a fire, nylon melts on to the skin.)

You should not, by the way, expect to stay in an emergency exit seat, should a problem emerge during your flight, even if you start out occupying one. I was flying home from America on one occasion and was seated at an emergency exit, although back then you didn't have to pay extra for the ability to stretch your legs out. I was fast asleep, as were most of the passengers, when the pilot told us that we were to wake up, sit up and listen up. He said that the cockpit was on fire, somewhere, although it wasn't clear precisely where, and that instead of heading for Dublin, as he was booked to, he was going to – quote – 'Try to make Shannon'. He was also going to take the plane down to ten thousand feet to vent the cockpit.

So I'm sitting in this plane, possibly the most grimly well-informed passenger in it, when a steward appears beside me with a man who looks like a weight lifter.

'Ma'am, do you have the physical capability to move a fifty-six pound door?' she demanded.

I shook my head.

'Then you must leave your seat and this gentleman will take it,' she said. 'Follow me.'

I gathered my stuff and followed her down the aisle, watching the other passengers as I proceeded. Some were trembling, weeping and clutching each other. Some had gone back to sleep. Now, before you decide that they were incredibly confident, let me tell you the reverse may be the case. Some people, when desperately fearful, go to sleep. Racing drivers have been known to nod off at the starting line. Some had fallen asleep on the basis that there was damn all they could do to affect the outcome, so why not go back to blissful unconsciousness? Some had fallen asleep through fear. Oddly, one woman I passed was lashing into a package of sandwiches she had saved. If this plane was going to go down, she was going to have plenty of personal fuel for rescue purposes.

I settled into the seat vacated by the weight lifter and considered my options. We were more than halfway across the Atlantic, which argued that if the pilot could keep the plane in the air, the chances were reasonably good that we would make it as far as Shannon. I considered writing a letter to my husband on my hand in indelible pen and decided against it. He knew I loved him, and prospective post-mortem declarations seemed in bad taste. The girl in the seat beside me began to chat and in no time at all, we had created a little comedy coven down our end of the plane, which, serendipitously, was the back end, so – as far as was known at the time – my survival prospects were statistically improved over the man whose seat I had taken. Except of course, as we now know, his chances were improved by being at an exit door. You win some, you lose some.

There was a faint whiff of smoke in the cabin, but only a faint whiff. As we came closer to the coast of Ireland and dawn coldly revealed the bleak sea, the cabin crew said nothing to us. Neither did the pilot. I didn't know whether to think badly of them for not keeping up passenger morale or to be grateful that they were concentrating on flying the bloody plane.

When we landed in Shannon, fire tenders raced alongside the plane until it came to a halt, then covered it with foam. Eventually, they let us out and we disembarked carefully, stepping over hoses and water seeping from the cockpit. It was at this point that passengers who had held it together admirably up to that completely lost it. The weeping and gnashing of teeth at every telephone was something to behold.

I learned later that the pilot had telephoned his wife and his mother to say goodbye to them. He'll probably never fly again. because he was at the time in his late fifties. If a crisis like that happens to a young pilot, it becomes a war story. Not a war story for an older pilot.

So the end result was that at least one passenger on the flight (me) became less fearful of flying, whereas the pilot may have developed a deep fear of flying.

The fact is that flying is safe, not least because of all the checklists that have to be gone through before take-off is authorised. It's more difficult – as we all know to our cost – to get on a plane carrying a potential weapon. Every passenger aircraft has to pass a test to show it can be emptied in ninety seconds.

The biggest danger you face, in the event of an emergency on board, is the irrational behaviour of other human beings. Some passengers freeze, even when they desperately need to be up and moving. Some are motivated by social bonds with other passengers – adults tend to help children escape, for example. In addition, passengers seem to be more likely to comply with cabin crew instructions in a test than in a real emergency.

Aerophobia is a continuum. Some sufferers will never cross an airbridge. Ever. Some will do it under duress. One well-known journalist lives in daily dread of a story that will require her to go to another country. (She's also phobic about elevators and bridges. You'd think life as a hack was interesting enough without adding all those complications, wouldn't you?)

Another phobic can list the three air journeys he has survived: 'Isle of Man, Jersey and Shannon.' I forgot to ask him why he flew to Shannon, but he evidently chickened out of flying back.

'I spent every journey looking at the rivets in the wings, wondering when they were going to pop,' he admits. 'I had this total conviction that the seats were going be sucked out from under us all, and I was trying to work out what I could grab above me when that happened. I think the reason I suffer from fear of flying is that I'm so not in control of my situation in a plane. I'm never driven in a car. I drive myself everywhere. In a plane, I have no control whatever. OK, if I had a sick child in Australia, I'd get on a plane. But for any other reason? No. Being flown by someone else and being told to sit down in your seat…It's not a preference, though. It's a phobia. I mean, even when I took the short flight to Jersey for a holiday, years ago, a friend's wife gave me Valium to take before I got on the plane. Two of them. And I had a couple of brandies, too. But even then, we hit air pockets on the journey and dropped like about a thousand feet at one stage and I remember it vividly. If I could wear a parachute on my back the whole time, I wouldn't feel so bad. Although going over the sea I'd need a wee canoe as well.'

Being aerophobic evidently takes up a lot of thinking time. Oh, and when two aerophobics get together, they tell jokes about crises in the air:

'So Paddy and Cathy are flying to America and the pilot comes over the intercom. "As you may have noticed," he says, "One of the engines on the right wing is on fire. This is nothing to worry about. We have three other engines that are fine. It just means we'll be an hour later, getting into New York." Ten minutes later, he comes back on. "Passengers on the left side of the plane will have noticed that an engine on their side is on fire. No worries – it just means we'll be two hours later than planned, getting into JFK." A little more time elapses before he interrupts the movie a third time, to announce that a third engine has flamed out, which means the flight will be three hours late. Paddy turns to his wife and says, "Jasus, if the fourth engine goes, we'll be up here all night."

(I didn't say it was funny. Just that it's the kind of joke aerophobics tell each other. Remember, they're stressed out to start with. Is it any wonder their sense of humour suffers from metal fatigue?)

If you're already even a teeny weeny bit aerophobic, you would not want to read transcripts of the black box recordings recovered from downed aircraft, but they're fascinating. My favourite comes from a United Airlines flight in the summer of 1989. At 37,000 feet, one of the engines broke apart, propelling bits of metal into the body of the plane, where they played hell with the hydraulics. Captain Al Haynes suddenly found himself with virtually no controls functioning. It was, he has said, like racing a car down a mountain trying to steer and slow down by opening and closing the doors. That bad.

'Folks, I'm not gonna kid anybody,' he told the passengers. 'This is gonna be rough.'

'This' was the prospect of landing in Sioux City, Iowa, when all the crew could get the plane to do was sweeping right-hand turns.

Now, what the crew didn't know was that the air-traffic controller in Sioux City, who was so calmly dealing with an unfolding horror in the skies above him, was actually on his first week in the job. He'd left an air traffic control post in New York because he had found it too stressful.

'You're cleared to land on any runway,' the controller coolly told Captain Haynes, minutes before the inevitable catastrophe. And you know the fantastic thing? Haynes's response was a laugh at the assumption in the instruction.

'Roger,' he said. 'You want to be particular and make it a runway, huh?'

Then he landed the DC10 as best he could. It cartwheeled as it hit, broke up and burst into flames. Yet almost two-thirds of the passengers got out, including a baby whose crying caused a passenger who had already escaped the burning fuselage to go back in, find and rescue her. Al Haynes, the man who had been able to joke in the final seconds of a flight he expected to kill him, came out alive.

Although he's as heroic in his calm as Captain Sullenberger, the pilot involved in the miracle on the Hudson in 2009, Haynes is not unusual, in his focus on detail in an aviation crisis. The black box recordings tend to reveal that the pilots in such a situation focus is on what they're doing, not on any dire possibilities. They work, they help each other, they inform ground control, and then, in the last few seconds when disaster becomes inevitable, the voice recorders almost always catch them saying a variant of 'Oh, shit.' And that's it.

Many organisations, including airlines, provide pro-grammes to help people overcome a phobia about flying. These programmes usually follow a pattern of gradual desen-sitisation, so that over time, the phobic gets nearer and nearer the plane.

One such organisation, based in Dublin and run by

Michael Comyn, is flyfearless.com. They do seminars and longer programmes, have their own simulator and claim that more than 90 per cent of their graduates now fly regularly and without phobic fear.

Fear of Getting Points on Your Driver's Licence

RSA Chairman Gay Byrne would believe you definitely should be afraid of points and pretty damn ashamed if you get some. Dammit to hell, all you have to do is stay within the speed limit, get your car to the NCT centre, stay sober and get enough sleep. How hard is that?

Well, according to *Schott's Almanac*, one of those yearly instalment encyclopaedias of unlikely information, your choice of music might contribute to your car gaining enough speed to tip you over the limit. Here's what it has to say:

'Drivers who listen to blues music are most likely to get caught speeding, according to a May 2008 survey by Saga Motor Insurance. Country music fans are second most likely to speed, followed by reggae devotees. The most popular driving songs: "Bat out of Hell" by Meatloaf; "Bohemian Rhapsody" by Queen; "Born to be Wild" by Steppenwolf; "Don't stop Me Now" by Queen, "Hotel California" by the Eagles.'

11

Fear of Bugs, Common Or Garden: Entemophobia

When I was a kid, I had a pecking order for bugs. Probably should have been called a crawling order but that's a side issue. My list was a Top Twenty of the insect world. Starting with acceptability and working down, it went something like this:

1. Butterflies
2. Ladybirds
3. Spiders
4. Earwigs
5. Centipedes
6. Ants
7. Greenfly
8. Bees
9. Beetles
10. Moths
11. Daddy Long Legs
12. Houseflies
13. Bluebottles
14. Maggots
15. Woodlice
16. Mosquitoes
17. Ticks
18. Bedbugs
19. Wasps
20. Cockroaches

A number of years later, the list holds up, although I'd be open to negotiation on a few of the middle-ranging lads in there. Like most lists, including those starring denizens of the deep, it starts with the prettiest and works down.

The top-of-the-class-kiss-teacher position of the butterfly is impregnable, even if they arrive at their glory days having come from the caterpillar stage. Next in line are ladybirds. It's easy to love ladybirds, although you have to figure that the Americans love them less than we do, because they call them 'ladybugs'. Anything that dresses up so well just to go out and work at eating greenfly has to have a good attitude. Greenfly are called greenfly to confuse people, because they actually come in a range of colours, including brown. What's cute about greenfly is that they come with their own drinking straw to suck the sap out of plants. This is not good for the plants – ask any rose-grower. Greenfly suck up so much sap that they exude it in a foam L'Ecrivain's chef would be proud of. Park underneath a tree inhabited by greenly and you will soon know all about this innate capacity, because blobs of the goo will fall off onto your car, where they're as noticeable and sticky as discarded chewing gum.

Rose-growers and lettuce-producers may not like greenfly, but the insect has its fans. One brand of ant has worked out that if they hang around aphids (that's the technical term for greenflies) they will be able to feast for free on the sweet foam they produce. Birds, particularly blue tits, prey on greenfly, but the hero of the war against the aphid is the ladybird. You can now buy ladybird breeding stations from some of the ecology shops, if you prefer to outsource your aphid-assassination, although DIY murder is possible using a few drops of Quix diluted in water and sprayed on the plants, or, if the infestation is severe and you're not really that pushed about having your roses organic, chemical extermination spray.

Arachnophobia, one of the most common and pronounced insect fears, relates to spiders. I suspect race memory of the tarantula and a couple of its oversized tropical cousins makes people scared of spiders, but if you have this fear, you are wrong and I won't even tell you about the spider-killing spray you can buy from American catalogues.

Spiders are good. They trap and do away with bad bugs inside your house, and if you go outside on a frosty morning you can see how hard they work at decorating your hedge. In addition, folk medicine suggests that putting a cobweb on a wound helps healing. I did intend to test this one out before publishing the book but I didn't get wounded as often as I expected while writing it. It's not that writing books, in and of itself, is dangerous. It's just that I'm accident-prone.(And please, please don't make a punning joke about my name. I've suffered that joke every time I've ended up in hospital, starting on my fourth birthday.) There is no accident of which I am not capable. Driving, I've hit a tree, a jeep, a van carrying sausage rolls (pastry flakes everywhere) a rubbish skip, a statue of Our Lady in the middle of a roundabout and a car driven by a man I had to interview on radio ten minutes after giving him whiplash. I've fallen off horses, bicycles, skates, beds and platform shoes. I can even fall up stairs.

But I managed to get through the past months without stabbing or slicing myself, which is just as well, because when you've just inflicted a gaping wound upon yourself is not the time to go looking for cobwebs. I wouldn't be the tidiest around the house but I'd be quicker at finding an elastoplast than a spider's web, especially if I were bleeding profusely at the time. So I cannot personally vouch for the efficacy of spider's webs on a cut.

I do, however, believe that fear and loathing of spiders is counter-intuitive and doesn't make a lot of sense. They don't bite, they don't want to make friends with you, they don't carry disease. In fact, they exterminate bugs that do carry disease. And yet, starting with Miss Muffet, we demonise spiders. Even the Miss Muffet rhyme shows unjustified spider prejudice. All he does is arrive while she's eating her curds and whey. He doesn't want any of it. (I suspect she didn't want any of it, either, but cornflakes hadn't been invented, back then.) He doesn't interfere with her in any way, yet she abandons her tuffet in a panic.

The only disadvantage I can see to peaceful coexistence with spiders is that, unless you take a long-handled duster to where the walls join the ceiling, you can end up with a house that looks like Miss Haversham's, but other than that, spiders do no harm, which is why, even though they evoke irrational fear, we have them close to the top of the insect hate parade.

Earwigs run them close. Earwigs are those fast-moving little guys with the pincers on their tails and quite sensible people like my husband come over all funny if you even mention an earwig, never mind presenting one to them. If my husband sees an earwig, he goes berserk. Nothing will hold him back. The rest of the world can go to hell in a hand-basket while he becomes Lord High Executioner of one small and objectively harmless creepie crawlie. He explains, 'I suppose it goes back to childhood, when you were told they'd go into your ear and wreck your head. I felt that as a young fella and it has never gone away.'

Centipedes, to my mind, are cute, although I have never been able to persuade my mother of this. When my big sister, Hilary, was only a baby, my mother encountered a centipede in the house, which was way out in the country in a wooded stretch of farmland called Tallaght. My mother wrapped up my sister, put her in the pram, left a note for my father to read when he cycled home from work, instructing him to do a search and destroy and find a way to confirm her of centipede destruction before she would return to the marital abode. Then she locked the house and walked ten miles, pushing the pram, to her mother's house, leaving the centipede in complete control of the property. It could be said that he was briefly the precursor of NAMA.

Ants, on the other hand, were greatly admired by my mother, partly because someone gave her, early on, a copy of Maurice Maeterlinck's *The Life of the Ant*, a fascinating account of the insect which I still have. But I suspect the real reason she was so approving of ants was that their diligence appealed to her. Ants don't kick back much. They have a powerful sense of the common good and they work, well, like ants. All day, every day.

Inheriting my mother's unquestioning approval of the ant kingdom made me miss the fact that they come in different brands. There are soldier ants, carpenter ants, grease ants and pavement ants. The latter have been observed in New York, breaking concrete into grains to take it away and use for construction purposes elsewhere. A bit like the way scavengers will take the odd bit of copper piping from one building to benefit another and maybe in the process benefit their own finances, too.

Because of inherited ant approval, when my son was about four and on holiday in Florida, he welcomed a particularly large ant on to his hand, which the ant then stung with enormous enthusiasm. It was a fire ant and fortunately – and untypically – was on its own, because a collective attack by fire ants can be horrific and even fatal. Anton has had a nuanced view of ants since then, and an even more nuanced view of what his mother tells him about interspecies trust. Or anything else.

Bees are noisy – remember Yeats's 'bee-loud glade'? – but necessary. They also produce honey, which tastes awful, in my view, but is a great emergency antiseptic. This may be because it contains traces of hydrogen peroxide, which research suggests might give it some medicinal benefits. Scientists in Aintree Hospital, Liverpool and the University of Wales have found that manuka honey can help in the fight against MRSA when it's applied to wounds. It may or may not have been that kind of honey that was buried with Tutankhamun so he'd have something to scoff on his way to whatever bit of the afterlife is reserved for Egyptian pharaohs. Those who excavated his tomb maintained that his pot of honey was still edible. The contents, I mean. Which does rather bring into question those 'best by' dates on the bottom of more recent jars of honey –

they're hardly relevant if the stuff lasts through millennia. Although this level of preservation might happen only in royal tombs: 'Store in a cool, dry place, close to a mummy.'

Even occasional stings may have medicinal properties – some arthritis sufferers maintain that a few bee stings will greatly reduce the symptoms of their particular auto-immune crippler. In short, if you're afraid of bees but aren't physically allergic to them, bluntly, you're going to have to get over it, because the bee is a threatened species in several parts of the world, for a variety of unrelated reasons. The Varroa mite entered Britain in 1992 and played hell with the British wild bee population. In Argentina, the honey bee population has been damaged by droughts. But that's not all. The Argentinian bee has also suffered because of the conversion of land to the growth of soya beans for biofuel. (No good environmental deed goes unpunished.) Go a bit north and a mysterious 'colony collapse disorder' has been blamed for the death of 36 per cent of American honey bees.

All of this is bad news – even potentially fatal news – for humanity. Bees contribute heavily to the worldwide economy by pollinating fruits and vegetables, which is why Albert Einstein once observed: 'If the bee disappears off the surface of the globe, then man would only have four years of life left.'

If you know you have a tendency to develop anaphylactic shock when stung by a bee, wear long sleeves and repellent when out of doors, don't wear coloured patterns that would confuse it into thinking you were a flower, or perfumes/ shampoos with fruit or flower essences in them, for the same reason. If you don't suffer this reaction, leave bees alone, no matter how much they frighten you. You need them.

Beetles are neither here nor there and moths are annoying because they make bees look like stripy Einsteins by comparison with their total stupidity. Back in the days of candles, moths would always fly into them and get incinerated. You'd think they'd learn, although if we're to be fair-minded, I suppose you have to acknowledge that the dead ones couldn't come back to tell the live ones to watch out for those sticky-up yokes with the light on top.

One particular version of these annoying discount-store butterflies, the clothing moth, eats wool, or rather, its caterpillar does. A moth larva won't eat live wool on the hoof, so to speak, instead preferring to get itself outside a meal of jumper, fur or even a feather or two. It would not, however, be seen dead eating synthetic fibres. Polyester will not pass its lips. A touch of class, this moth has, although if you wallop it with a folded magazine, which I know you wouldn't – you being afraid of those animal liberation folk – it's unnerving to find that, instead of the bloody squelch you get when you hit most bugs, what you get if you hit a clothing moth is dust.

Before synthetic fibres were developed, the larva of the clothing moth was a constant threat to everyone's winter woollies, which, if you weren't lucky enough to own cotton underpants, included wool versions of them and of vests, the itchiness of which, according to older relatives, had to be scratched to be believed. Because of this threat (holes in your knickers, not itchiness) our grandparents used to store their clothes with mothballs. This made them smell peculiar in the springtime. The habit, in turn, gave rise to the association of passive storage with mothballs, giving rise to the weird phrases particularly beloved of the US Navy, which is always talking about 'mothballing' aircraft carriers and warships generally.

Mothballs are still available, but have a number of disadvantages, including smell, the possibility of their being carcinogenic and the likelihood of poisoning small children and pets if they get to like the (apparently) sweet taste. As well as mothballs, an earlier generation swore by storing their woollies in cedar boxes or drawers, cedar containing an oil that kills off clothing moth larva. However, it does it only to a particular age of larva, which limits the use of cedar, although the scent is more pleasing than that of mothballs.

These days, if you're in a moth zone, the simplest preventive measure is to put your woollies (and furs and feathers) in a plastic storage box with a lid that excludes air. Keeping your clothing clean helps, too. Clothing moths apparently prefer their wool a bit manky and sweaty. If they find themselves in a home where not only are the clothes kept clean but where some of the available wool has never been worn at all, because it's owned by a knitter, they will get promiscuous and eat whatever's available. Nobody knows for sure but knitters have always believed that stashing bunches of lavender in with the balls of wool protects them. Others maintain that spraying the wool with a tea made of any of the following herbs – rosemary, lavender, thyme or ginseng – will do the same. Which explains why, in that song, Simon and Garfunkel kept nagging whoever was going to Scarborough Fair to bring back parsley, sage, rosemary and thyme. It wasn't all destined for the cooking pot.

The housefly ranking on the ladder of rejectable insects marks the point at which we move from the innocent-until-proven present kind to the guilty-for-just-existing kind. The housefly is useful to predators and can walk upside-down on the ceiling and that's all that can be said about the housefly in the way of positives. The bluebottle is a housefly on steroids wearing a metallic uniform and boasting about it noisily. The housefly and the bluebottle walk around on cow pats, then fly into your home and walk around on your kitchen surfaces and any food thereon.

Houseflies and bluebottles generate the next fearful thing: maggots. A maggot is the larval stage of a bluebottle or fly before it fully matures and you rarely meet a maggot on its own. They're social, and the mother fly lays all her eggs in one basket. Or wherever she picks to lay them. I one opened a dustbin and found it contained a sluggishly moving porridgy mass of off-white maggots. It's not an experience you'd choose to repeat.

Which is not to say that maggots don't have their good points. Very useful, maggots can be, except that where they can be of most use – in a hospital setting – spoilsports dedicated to cleanliness won't even consider them. Back in the days of the American Civil War, it was discovered that putting maggots on a wound allowed them to eat away all the gangrenous tissue, leaving the wound clean as could be, in a much less painful way than the process of scraping, called 'debriding' the nurses otherwise had to do.

Fans of CSI know that maggots are also forensically invaluable, as their size and condition can establish how long a murdered body has lain in the open.

None of these uses takes away the horror most people experience at the very thought of a maggot. However, it is possible to encounter them by accident and to quite like them. One of the legends of our family concerns a distant relative and the distant relative's mother, who was aged and had lost her sight. The distant relative, let's call her Jane, was reading to her mother one evening when a power cut happened. The two of them chatted for a while, considering the options open to them for entertainment in the dark, which weren't many. They knew they had candles but, as always happens in a power cut, the people in the house couldn't quite remember where the candles were, and anyway they'd need light to go searching in drawers.

'I'm hungry,' the mother eventually said. 'D'you know what I'd love?'

'What would you love?'

'Semolina. I haven't had semolina for ages.'

Now, if you have eaten semolina, a milky pudding of prize-winning viscosity and blandness, you might think the old lady's semolina-free life was tickety-boo and that she shouldn't reintroduce herself to it. But apparently a long-buried yearning for semolina, is, like yawning, kind of contagious, so Jane began to think a bowl of semolina would be a delightful change from their normal supper. Plus, she remembered exactly where the packet of semolina was in the press and their gas hob would more or less provide its own light, as well as heat. So off she went into the kitchen, guessed roughly the right amount of milk to add to the saucepan and lit the jet under it, by which she would be well able to cook the pudding. Which she did, unhampered by the fact that the light from the jet didn't reach and illuminate the inside of the saucepan. Two bowls were duly served, jet turned off, and she and her mother started to spoon their semolina in the dark. It tasted better than Jane had expected. It even tasted better than her mother remembered.

'This is the best semolina I've ever eaten,' Jane's mother remarked.

At that moment the lights came back on and Jane found herself looking at a bowl filled with semolina and cooked maggots. She ran for the bathroom. When she returned, her mother had finished the bowl and wondered aloud if there was any left in the saucepan. At which point Jane had an ethical discussion with herself. She could upset her mother by telling the blind old lady that she was now the container for cooked maggots, which she had totally enjoyed, or feed her more of them. She fed her the remainder, and her mother talked for weeks about the unexpected delights of semolina consequent upon a power cut.

Woodlice are like grey maggots with corrugated backs and they hang around anywhere that's damp. Which means that the first thing people (including me) who own Martello Towers do when they meet each other is check how bad the other owner's woodlice problem is. Nobody seems to have worked out a way to get rid of them. Kittens do their fair share of extermination, but as the kittens get bigger, they get bored with the slow pace of the average woodlouse and move on to bigger prey that can give them a better run for their miaow.

Mosquitoes and ticks, unlike woodlice, are a real and present danger to the life and health of most of the world and the bad news is that climate change is bringing a mosquito close to where you live, possibly transporting a major disease with it.

Malaria is one of the oldest diseases around and played a considerable role in bringing some civilisations to a grinding halt. The ancient Romans associated it rightly with the swamps where mosquitoes bred but attributed it wrongly to the bad air around those swamps, from which it got its name. When they arrived in America, Jesuit missionaries learned from indigenous tribes that a preparation brewed up from the bark of a particular tree helped to reduce the ghastly fevers associated with malaria. To this day, the chemical, quinine, which the priests learned to extract from tree bark, is used to treat the illness.

Towards the end of the nineteenth century, scientists began to figure out that the blood of malaria-sufferers carried a parasite. Where it came from wasn't established until 1897, when a British officer named Ronald Ross, working in India, worked out that the mosquito could pick up the parasite when it bit a human and act as a transport system, bringing it to other humans as well as to parrots and any other species a mosquito chose to bite. He immortalised his discovery in a poem:

> ... With tears and toiling breath,
> I find thy cunning seeds,
> O million-murdering Death.

(Not impressed? Me neither. But he was a scientist, remember. Poem-production was just a nixer as far as he was concerned.)

One of the best weapons against the 'million-murdering Death' for which the mosquito served as An Post was an insecticide called DDT. It came in a tower-like drum and could be sprinkled wherever mosquitoes or other insects laid their eggs or hung around. It was remarkably effective. So effective that medical missionary Albert Schweitzer wrote about it in his autobiography: 'How much labour and waste of time these wicked insects do cause us,' he noted. 'But a ray of hope is now held out to us in the use of DDT.'

Then along came a biologist and zoologist named Rachel Carson. In 1962, Carson published the book that effectively started the twentieth century environmental movement. Its title was *Silent Spring*, which was more than a poetic name for a new book. It was based on research Carson had done which established that when a mosquito or other insect ingested a bit of DDT and was subsequently eaten by a bird, it thinned the shells of the eggs the bird later laid. If this continued, Carson's speculations suggested, the end result would be that birds would lay eggs with shells so tissue-paper thin that they would be destroyed in the birth canal or when the mother bird sat down on them to keep them warm before the chicks inside hatched. And if that happened, the consequence was inevitable: some spring, humanity would look around as the days started to lengthen, and there would be no birdsong, because there would be no little birds.

That realisation changed everything. Not immediately. Directly after the books was published, the big chemical companies producing insecticides threw their considerable resources into an attack on the naturalist, portraying her as an hysterical woman who wasn't qualified to write such a book and claiming that she had been exceedingly selective in the evidence she presented. A germ of truth was to be found in the latter allegation, but it was Carson's time, and as public opinion moved against the chemical giants, DDT was banned. Which banning gave the mosquito a new lease of life. Other pesticides have been developed since the banning which are very effective but the relentless march of malaria is sometimes bitterly attributed to the removal of the key preventive weapon, DDT.

As the globe warms, it is predicted that the mosquito will move north into territories once too cold for it, bringing malaria and an assortment of other diseases with it. We may all have to wear long-sleeved shirts, spray ourselves with repellent and light citronella candles in the back garden in just a few years' time. In the interim, anybody travelling to the tropics should get the appropriate prophylactic and take it faithfully in advance of and during their visit, because the mosquito is a serious and a smart enemy of which we should be very, very, afraid.

The tick may not have quite the killing history of is the mosquito, but it's a nasty little customer, too, which can carry a horrible illness called Lyme Disease. This is one of those stinker ailments that starts with a rash and a ring of inflamed skin around where the tick bite was located. Other symptoms at this stage include headache and swollen lymph nodes. It progresses to damage the heart and the nervous system. It creates severe arthritis in joints and is associated with depression and anxiety. Understandably.

Fear of mosquitoes and ticks is not enough. Either go somewhere they don't go, or use every available method of keeping yourself free from them.

While we're on the subject of insects that are doing better than we are in the changing conditions within which we live, let us look at the bedbug. Oh, come on, you know you want to.

'Bed bugs are becoming a significant problem in Ireland and around the world. They are easily spread and difficult to treat, resulting in a rapid growth in the number of bed bug outbreaks. The key to beating this problem is to raise awareness of bed bugs, to know how to get rid of bed bugs and to ensure bed bugs are dealt with quickly once discovered.'

So say Rentokil, the guys who go up your pipes and down your tubes to eliminate household pests. You'd expect them to be intimate with the bed bug, and they don't deny it. In fact, they know it so well they can tell you it changes shape and colour after it has had its dinner. Pre-meal, it's oval and pale. After dinner, it's round and dark.

Bed bugs used to be so constant a nocturnal reality that people would put the legs of their beds in buckets of water in an attempt to stop the bugs reaching them. Dr John O'Connell, once Minister for Health, was persuaded, in his early days as a newly-qualified doctor, to work in the Dublin slums by a Jewish doctor who took him to see the squalor of the living conditions of the poor at the time. The two doctors stood in the open doorway of the bedroom of a dying man and as they were about to enter the room, the other doctor halted Dr John, pointing to the floor where a living grey carpet had begun to move away from the bed. That meant, the other doctor explained, that the man was dead. The parasitic bedbugs would leave in search of another victim the moment they sensed their current supplier had died.

Despite tricks like buckets of water, bed bugs were an ever-present torment, to such an extent that the sign-off for the day with children was often 'Good night, sleep tight. Don't let the bed bugs bite.'

When they bite, it's not painful, but the bite becomes severely itchy and when a full-scale infestation happens it can cause a rash.

As affluence spread and overcrowding diminished, as hot water was available on tap and homes became more clean, most nations saw a retreat of the bed bug. But – as Rentokil confirms – they're making a comeback. So big a comeback that hotels and motels across America are fighting hard not to inflict them on their paying guests. Frequent business travellers are taking their own measures: one of the best-selling items from online stores selling travel goods is a silk sleeping bag which can be slipped between the sheets of a hotel bed and which has a flap to cover the pillow, so the sleeper never comes into direct contact with the bed linen, no matter how well laundered it may be.

In 2010, the *Guardian* reported that, this time around, the resurgent bed bugs are not a product of poverty but of wealth and travel, with frequent fliers bringing them home in their luggage from infested hotels. Nor do the bed bugs confine themselves to sleeping places. A couple of New York cinemas (no doubt showing movies about the horror of gigantic bugs taking over the city) added to the experience of their audiences by having them bitten by these bugs.

If you fear bedbugs, the best advice is to keep your home clear of them and stay in it. Because – I am told – few experiences are less joyful than squashing a bug and realising that the blood you've spilled is your own.

One of the most joyful experiences of my recent years has been overcoming my fear of wasps. This might suggest I have no life but I am proud of myself, nonetheless. Having been stung as a child, I have always regarded wasps as vicious, evil and overdressed. If a bee stings you, the bee is desperate or confused and will die as a result. If, on the other hand, a wasp stings you, it does it out of malice and can go on to sting dozens of other people, because wasps do nothing useful and they know it, so they're filled with spite and venom.

Throughout my life, whenever a wasp appeared, I entered panic mode. No words, just shrieks, moans and fruitless flapping. For the most part, this had the unconsciously desired effect: someone would remove or kill the wasp and all would be well. A few years ago, though, I realised that those closest to me saw my performance as ridiculous. My husband viewed it as an unfortunate characteristic, like short-sightedness. My son regarded it as a ridiculous get-over-it. So I decided to get over it. Present me with a wasp and I take calm, considered action. Once I did it the first time, I convinced myself I could always do it. Sooner or later, a wasp is going to sting me to prove I was right, back in the panic days, but since I don't suffer from anaphylactic shock reaction, that's not going to kill me.

The most hated, most interesting yet relatively harmless bug is the cockroach. I thought for a long time that my mother was the only person with a cockroach obsession. That was before I met John Lonergan, the former Governor of Mountjoy Jail. Before Mr Lonergan retired from the job, one of his prisoners took an unsuccessful court case seeking release. The prisoner didn't seem to have a problem sharing the premises with miscreants, muggers, murderers and child molesters, but he drew the line at mice and cockroaches.

Not long afterwards, I happened to meet the then Governor of the prison and couldn't resist raising the cockroach issue with him. Now, John Lonergan had a well-earned reputation for quiet passion on behalf of his prisoners and personal pride in his staff. His interviews on radio and television are characterised by gentle firmness and caring humanity.

None of which extends to cockroaches. Say 'cockroach' to John Lonergan and stand well back, because that word reveals in him an unrecognised abusive fluency. There is no cockroach alive he doesn't personally hate. There's nothing he doesn't know about the methods available for their extermination. John Lonergan and my mother head up the Hate Cockroach Society in Ireland.

Madonna, on the other hand, seems to be a fan. 'I am a survivor,' she has claimed. 'I am like a cockroach, you just can't get rid of me.'

Cockroaches have been around a lot longer than mankind, and have been remarkably successful, as a species. They go back three-hundred-and-fifty million years. Specimens that are five million years old have been found, preserved in aspic, and they're not very different from the ones we have today. Sorry. The ones you have today. I may be a slob but I'm a clean slob, so I've never encountered a cockroach. In Ireland, that is. In Florida, it's a whole other bug game but over there, they've applied the principles of PR to cockroaches. They've rebranded them. They call them palmetto bugs. Sounds better, doesn't it?

Five years ago, Britain's Natural History Museum set up the first online cockroach database. George Beccaloni, a cockroach expert at the Museum, assembled the database from a 1224-page catalogue published in sections between 1862 and 1971, which argues that several generations of scholarly Britons have paid a lot more attention to the cockroach than my mother and John Lonergan would think acceptable.

The Madonna of the insect world, according to the Natural History Museum, can go without food for a month and manage without air for nearly an hour. It can survive freezing and radiation better than humans can, although the belief that, in the aftermath of a nuclear holocaust, cockroaches would be the only species remaining alive, is not supported by the evidence. A lot of bugs would survive irradiation better than us humans but cockroaches have no unique capacity in this regard. They can, however, live for several days after decapitation. If they still have their heads but are put in a situation where food is scarce, they will eat glue or each other. They are extremely intelligent, and can recognise smells like vanilla and peppermint as signifying that edibles are around here somewhere.

Dr Hananel Davidowitz of the NEC Research Institute in Princeton, New Jersey, has analysed the avoidant speed of the cockroach and worked out that it thinks with its behind. Which may explain why it can survive so long without its head. Davidowitz's research, published in *Nature* magazine, establishes that the cockroach can sense minute changes in the air flowing round its body using tiny hairs on two posterior appendages called 'cerci.' Signals from these hairs are processed by nerve cells which alert their owner to impending threat. The only thing capable of subverting this sophisticated warning system is the vacuum cleaner, which confuses the hell out of the information-gatherers on the cockroach posterior, so it thinks the threat is ahead, not behind, and goes rushing towards the machine that's going to hoover it up.

One particular kind of wasp stings the cockroach at a particular point on its back, a bit like the way picadors weaken the bull before the matador starts his performance by sticking small daggers into a vital part in the back of its neck. In the case of the cockroach, the sting paralyses it for five minutes, during which time the wasp delivers a second sting into the bit of its brain that governs the cockroach's escape reflex. The consequence is that, when it unfreezes from the paralysis, it makes no attempt to run away. The wasp drags it to its nest, where it lays an egg on it. When the egg develops into a larva, it feeds on the living, subdued cockroach. Which serves both of them right.

People's fear of the cockroach is not justified by their disease-carrying capacity. It was the flea, not the cockroach, that brought us the Black and several other plagues, yet we regard the flea as an embarrassment, rather than a terror. (And, should you ever need to catch a flea, think first of the soft side of a bar of soap.) They do tend to carry and disseminate materials damageing to asthmatics, plus they leave faeces around after them, but they don't carry bubonic plague or Lyme Disease. It doesn't matter. They could be as anti-septic as a bottle of Dettol and we'd still hate them.

Perhaps on the principle that the more you know about what you fear, the less fearful of it you will be, someone has developed an app for iPhone or iPad called iPest. Fans say that its coolest feature is a zoom option which allows you to get so close to the Australian cockroach that you can see it wears a Batman mask. Cute or what?

One American convict developed a meaningful relation-ship with a particular cockroach and even painted its little carapace in pleasing stripes – to ensure, one assumes, that the prisoner didn't waste his affections on the generality of cockroaches. Fidelity, in relationships, is important.

Unfortunately, one of the prison staff trod on the painted cockroach, thus stimulating the prisoner to sue. He eventually lost, because the expert lawyers brought in to oppose his case established that all prison cockroaches are the property of the state. (And there was John Lonergan destroying state assets, albeit not that successfully…)

12

Fear of Heights: Acrophobia

It was an event in London. Handily enough, the event was to happen in the hotel where participants were due to stay for the duration. No problem. Except when it came to booking the rooms. The room-booker got great prices for the seventeen people attending.

'And we're all on the same corridor,' she delightedly announced. 'On the twenty-second floor. Stunning views from every room.'

'Hmmm,' someone said.

The room booker began to look frazzled. 'What're you hmmming about?' she demanded.

'I'm really sorry and I should've said it in advance,' the hmmmer said, looking furtive. 'But I really have to be on the ground floor.'

'They've WiFi on all floors.'

'It's not really WiFi.'

'Well, what is it, then?'

'I can't handle heights.'

That stopped everybody in their tracks. This woman was the ablest and the toughest of the group. To find her afraid of anything was a revelation.

'How about the tenth floor?' someone suggested, which drove the room-booker nuts.

'No, it has to be the ground floor. I can't get into a lift.'

'Oh, that's why you always take the stairs. I thought it was for fitness.'

'So you couldn't do mountaineering?'

The acrophobe (fear of heights is called acrophobia) confided that she had once been driven around the Ring of

Kerry and had missed some of the most beautiful scenery in the world because she was a little bit busy, throwing up all the way into a SPAR bag.

'You want to know the whole truth? I can't go over a bridge that looks like a bridge.'

Work that one out. Apparently bridges in Dublin that look like bridges include the Ha'penny Bridge and the Samuel Beckett Bridge. The one bridge that doesn't look like a bridge is the O'Connell Bridge, because it's effectively a continuation of the road, without any hump in the middle, and it doesn't shift to one side, the way the Beckett Bridge does to accommodate tall ships. (The Samuel Beckett Bridge, as well as moving to one side, does a heart-stopping shimmy in a high wind.)

We didn't ask the staff member about bell-towers or the climbing of tall trees. We got the point. No getting around it. The acrophobe had to be on her own on the ground floor, which must have puzzled the hotel staff no end as they wondered what she had done to deserve being isolated twenty-one storeys below the rest.

She shares her real and genuine phobia with as much as 5 per cent of the population. Nearly twice as many women as men have this phobia. Fear of heights belongs to a group of phobias categorised as 'space and motion discomforts'.

The main symptoms can include the inability to move, the urge to cling on to something or someone, an urge to go down on all fours or descend as quickly as possible. Physically, the person may experience heart palpitations, shaking and sweating. You may not have witnessed an outbreak of such florid symptoms in anyone, but that's because sufferers avoid putting themselves in situations where they know they're going to begin to tremble and lose the full use of their limbs. Often the person involved will be convinced that they cannot move at all, even backwards away from the balcony ledge, for example.

Research undertaken by Russell Jackson, a cognitive

psychologist at California State University in San Marcos, shows another dimension to the condition. Dr Jackson's research indicates that in addition to the irrational fear of heights, his subjects seem to have a distorted perception of vertical distances. Along with the tendency to overestimate vertical distances, people with a fear of heights seem less able to call on vestibular cues (the ear canals) and rely too much on their already skewed visual cues. It's not that they were traumatised as a child by the height of their high chair, it's that their physical apparatus for detecting, sensing and reacting to balance is impaired.

Casting further doubt on the idea that the phobia may have been caused by a traumatic event involving heights, significant recent evidence has emerged that positions acrophobia as an inborn or non-associative fear. The non-association camp believe that the fear of heights is a trait left over from thousands of years of evolution, perhaps from a time when any fall was potentially fatal.

I regularly witness one of the funniest examples of fear of heights, clearly not caused by trauma. I live in a Martello Tower, which is open to the public on weekend mornings. When we excavated the tower, we discovered a water tank unlike any water tank you've ever seen. It was dug into the basement of the tower. If you think about the tower's inside as an orange cut in half and you then pulled out nearly a quarter of the orange, you have an idea of the scale of the reservoir. It is about five feet deep. It has a mortar floor and is bricked on all sides, thus allowing it to hold rainwater fed from the roof. If the tower had ever been besieged, the soldiers living in it wouldn't have been thirsty for quite a while.

We put heavy structural glass over the reservoir so people visiting the tower could walk across the space and get a good view of what was underneath. As soon as the glass was positioned and cleaned, we witnessed unexpected manifestations of fear of heights. Crawling toddlers, particularly one little girl named Joely, who had an enviable turn of speed on her tiny nappied bottom, loved it. It was extra slippery, so she could go faster. Once children hit the age of ten, however, they hesitated and had to have someone else demonstrate that the glass would sustain their weight. After which they were fine. Adults got the wobbles at the very idea of stepping onto it. Rationally, they knew that if the thing tipped them into the space, they would fall only a few feet. They also knew that: a) they were insured; and b) the glass could support a hundred times what they weighed. They watched me leaping enthusiastically on to it. Yet very few of them followed me.

'Yeah, no, you're grand,' was the typical response.

None of these people would regard themselves as acrophobics. None of them announced that they had experienced previous fear of heights. Most of them quite happily climbed the spiral staircase to the roof and surveyed the enormous view therefrom. But stepping on to nothingness over even a small drop terrified them.

Strangely, this pattern of young people being unafraid but older folk being terrified carried through to cats. Kittens danced fearlessly on to the glass. Adult cats let on to be bored by the very idea but whenever they thought nobody was looking, would essay a paw or two, eventually becoming confident with the height and pretending, as cats do, that they were always cool with it.

Any sort of movement or motion at a high level requires higher than usual visual processing. According to at least some of the experts in the field this high processing activity causes a bottleneck in the visual cortex, resulting in confusion and dizziness. Unlike some irrational fears, it is not always recommended that sufferers confront their fear of heights by actually placing themselves in a high situation in a bid to be released from it, as they may very well be unable to stop their natural urge to jump.

Just why some people are wired this way and others wired differently is unclear. From the late nineteenth century into the early twentieth century, when the great American skyscrapers were being constructed, the preferred workers were Native Americans, who were astonishingly sure-footed on scaffolding twenty storeys above ground level. It may have been an advantageous twist in their DNA. Or it may have been the belief that the earth was like a great magnet that sought to drag you down, and that, accordingly, you shouldn't get fixated on the distant earth. From father to son, the advice was the same.

'Don't look where you don't want to go,' they would remind one another.

Fear of Lifts

Sigourney Weaver may be able to cope with aliens, but when she's not in front of the camera, she's a wimp.

'In real life many things frighten me. Like taking elevators. I've been trapped in one a couple of times. I always check when it was last inspected.'

Good thinking. In fact, though, lifts are among the safest forms of transport around, and always have been. They have lots of 'redundancy' built into their systems, including buttons that allow you to summon help if the lift stops between floors. By the way, the myth that if you jump in the air just before a runaway lift hits bottom, you will survive, limbs unbroken, is just that: a myth. You'd be better to lie flat on the floor. If you had time. In the unlikely event of your lift losing the will to stay up.

The only time you should not get into a lift is in the case of fire. Most lifts carry this warning but American firefighters are given more specific data. They're told that the electronics within the lift may act as a heat-seeking missile, taking the lift to the floor that's alight, and opening the door into the conflagration.

All is not lost for the acrophobe wishing to be rid of her condition. Dr Brenda K. Wiederhold and her medical partners at the Virtual Reality Medical Centre in San Diego, California, have developed a whole medical centre for the sole purpose of curing people of their fear of heights. Their treatment involves creating a computer-generated virtual world and placing their patient within it. Here the acrophobe can 'experience' all the different stimuli through the wearing of specially designed TV monitors and standard stereo headphones. Unlike treating the patient in a potentially dangerous real-world situation, this advance in technology accurately recreates the stimuli that provoke anxiety and fear. What's more, the doctors can carefully increment the levels of fear-inducing stimuli so as not to 'over-frighten' the reluctant patient too hastily. This has proved a determining factor in convincing sufferers to seek rehabilitation and rid themselves of their phobia.

13

Fear of Open Spaces: Agoraphobia

In ancient Greece, the 'agora' was the marketplace, and so agoraphobia is fear of the marketplace or any open space. That does not mean that an agoraphobic would be terrified of being put in the middle of Croke Park or the Curragh, although they might be. It means that they would be terrified of a multitude of places. Agoraphobia is one of the most seriously disabling terrors, characterised by crippling panic attacks that can be triggered by fear of crowds, bridges, tunnels, long queues, or big buildings like airline terminals where the exits may not be immediately obvious because of the crowded complexity of the location.

The variety of symptoms attached to agoraphobia led Dr David V. Sheehan, a Professor at Harvard Medical School, to call it 'one of the great imposters in medical science'.

'Patients with this condition have usually visited many physicians over several years for relief,' he reports. 'The cardiologist may be consulted to investigate a rapid pulse, pounding heart, and chest pain; the neurologist for light-headedness and headaches; the ear, nose and throat specialist for a lump in the throat and dizziness; the gynaecologist for hot flushes; the endocrinologist for possible thyroid disease or low blood sugar; and the pulmonary specialist because of difficulty breathing or hyperventilation. Often the cancer specialist is consulted because of a preoccupation concerning malignant disease.'

One US hospital, in a study of agoraphobics, found that 70 per cent of them had been to ten or more doctors in the previous decade. It also found that the overwhelming majority of the sufferers were female and that many of them had a shared family history of similar symptoms.

Agoraphobia tends to appear out of nowhere, in people's late teens or early twenties. The sufferer suddenly gets a shocking onset of acute anxiety like nothing they have ever before experienced. They have to get out of wherever they are and some of them are convinced that if they don't, they will die.

The fact that the first panic attack has no warning and no rational explanation attached leaves the individual terrified that another will happen. If and when it does, they flee from the situation. It could be a big shop or a crowded public event. Ongoing anxiety attaches to that place, but because there's no logical reason for them to fear that particular site, the dread may widen: this awful experience could happen in any location, other than one's own home. Individuals suffering these horrible symptoms may avoid the situation or go to a particular place only when accompanied by a friend or relative. However, the consciousness that they are causing disruption to other lives and the interruptions to their own lives make them feel worthless and stupid. Consequently, the home becomes a refuge, to be left only with great reluctance.

Until our medicalised times, many agoraphobics may have been regarded simply as reclusive or eccentric. Every dynasty seems to have acknowledged that it had a member who 'kept to themselves,' never leaving their home, but it was regarded as an oddity, rather than an illness. For example, the poet Elizabeth Barrett Browning may have been agoraphobic. Before she met her poet husband, she stayed at home, lying on a couch in what seems to have been a form of self-induced paralysis, and even though she travelled with Robert Browning, once in a new location, she tended to stay in her adopted home, heavily tranquillised with laudanum. Agoraphobia tends to be complicated by other ailments and by ingestion of drugs. It is believed that Sigmund Freud, the father of psychoanalysis, was an agoraphobic. He was certainly a cocaine addict.

The condition was first described by the Austrian psychiatrist Carl Otto Westphal in 1871, when he wrote about a patient whose fear centred on one particular bridge.

'The appearance of the Dirschauer Bridge, where the curve had a wide span, was an uncomfortable experience,' Westphal recorded. 'During the times he had to cross it, a great feeling of anxiety overcame him, combined with the fear that he could become insane and would jump off the bridge during such a condition.'

It was Westphal who defined agoraphobia as 'fear of spaces,' to distinguish it from agrophobia (fear of open fields) and simple vertigo. He also realised that, for those who experience such fear, the boundaries of their own home can offer a sense of safety and security.

Westphal dealt with individual patients, but – exceptionally – a whole family in New York seem to have suffered from an agoraphobia which confined them for decades to a hotel. The Romero family were known as 'the hermits of Dream Street,' because Jose Romero de Cainas, his wife Michaela and their daughter Acacia came from Cuba and moved into a hotel on New York's West 47th Street in 1924. (The nickname 'Dream Street' derived from the brisk trade in narcotics conducted in the area around the hotel.)

The Romeros checked in. They never checked out. Unlike some recluses and agoraphobics, who can manage to get out of their residence under cover of darkness, the family simply never left the hotel suite. They never let anybody into the suite, either. Food and fresh linens were delivered to their door, as were newspapers. The hotel was handsomely paid for all services – by post from the Cuban sugar plantation owned by the family.

The first exception to the Romeros' 'No Entry' rule was an undertaker, whose services were required when the father of the family died. Just how the hotel found out is unclear, but lends itself to some grim guesswork. All that's known is that the manager told the wife and daughter he would not permit them to keep the body (as was their wish) but was calling the police. At which point they reluctantly allowed an undertaker to take away the body, but neither attended the funeral. They stayed put. The other exception was a plumber they had to let in to repair a leak in the bathroom. While he mended the pipe, the two women stood stock-still, facing a wall, both dressed in mourning black.

When the hotel owners decided to close the business in the 1940s, the manager at the time informed the two women. They refused to communicate with him and he had to haul in the Cuban consul to explain to them that they simply had to move to another nearby hotel. The two were now legendary in New York and newspaper reporters and photographers camped outside the hotel to catch a glimpse of them as they moved. So obsessive were the two that they never appeared, moving to the new hotel across the roof under cover of darkness, with the help of New York's Finest. After that, as the decades passed, media lost interest in them, and nobody knows how or when their tenancy of the second hotel ended.

Unlike the Romeros, who came from Cuba and were little known outside Dream Street, Howard Hughes, arguably the most famous agoraphobic in recent history, was world-famous during his lifetime. Like the Romeros, he was rich: a multimillionaire. The last man you'd expect to develop agoraphobia, Hughes was an industrialist, designer, aviator and film producer. When he died in 1976, he was worth more than $2 billion. The Texan was the son of a mining engineer who developed the first workable rotary drill for work on oil rigs. This made the father very rich. Howard inherited the father's machine tool company and built it into an empire.

But machine tools held his attention only for a period, after which he moved into film production and, as well as designing aircraft, he learned to fly. He set several speed records as a pilot and in 1938 flew around the world in ninety-one hours. He designed helicopters, satellites, missiles, a bra (for Jane

Russell, the film star) and a flying boat made from solid wood, called the Spruce Goose. It was supposed to become part of the defeat of the Nazis from the air, but the weight of the wood made this impracticable. The Spruce Goose did take to the air with Hughes at the controls. Once. After that, it went into a museum. A big museum, because the plane was vast.

Even as he progressed to owning RKO film studios and controlling Trans World Airlines, Hughes was making personal progress from oddity to eccentricity and from that to lunacy. As a handsome, glamorous and exceedingly rich young man, he had affairs with Katharine Hepburn, Bette Davis, Gene Tierney and Ava Gardner and married an actress named Jean Peters.

However, even in his early days, he had the seeds of a germ phobia which was to be a major factor in his later life. Getting into his car one day, Katharine Hepburn noticed something peculiar.

'What's that on the steering wheel?' she asked.

'Cellophane,' was his answer. 'If you had any idea of the crap that people carry around on their hands.'

'What kind of crap?'

'You don't wanna know.'

In fact, on this one, Howard Hughes was way ahead of his time. Microbiologists say that, because we sneeze into our hands, they become carriers of disease and that a handshake can transfer germs from one person to another. Food safety experts have a related take on the same issue, pointing out, for example, that if you handle raw chicken and immediately, without washing your hands, move on to handling cooked meat such as ham, you may transfer organisms from the raw meat which can make you or your family very ill indeed. But in Hughes's case, his concern about germs, even at an early stage, was sufficiently out of kilter with the norm to frustrate even Hepburn, who showered seven times a day. When she finally decided to get out of the relationship, he said to her: 'Actresses are cheap in this town, and I got a lot of money.'

Scott Fitzgerald's axiom that 'the rich are different' applied to Howard Hughes. Most of the people close to him in his younger days were financially dependent on him, so were unlikely to try to address his weird behaviours and beliefs. Even those who didn't work for him were dependent on him, his girlfriends because nobody else could show them quite such a good time, and others, including politicians, because of the money he donated to them.

'I don't want them bribed, Jack,' he told one of his servitors when the latter proposed a bribe to a politician. 'I want this done legal. I want them bought.'

It is of course, possible that some of those around him made allowances because of the fact that he was hard of hearing but the indications are that he himself was worried about his sanity long before anybody else seemed to register the loopy direction in which he was headed. He talked of his fear of losing his mind, muttering that it would be like a pilot flying blind.

As time went on and after at least one major air crash, his grasp of his company, his capacity to manage people and his ability to stay out of the law courts all diminished. He gradually withdrew from contact with former friends, holing up in hotel penthouses and moving only when circumstances demanded. So he spent five months at London's Inn on the Park, then a longer period in Nicaragua, and from 1966 to 1970 lived in the Desert Inn in Las Vegas.

As time went on, he communicated with the outside world only through his team of Mormons. He seems to have selected members of this Church because they were obedient, diligent and clean-living. The last characteristic was important to Hughes because of his germ phobia. Every door handle had to be wiped down with disinfectant several times a day.

He became increasingly obsessive-compulsive, with rituals around every aspect of his day. He also became addicted to codeine and other medications. In the last ten years, he abandoned clothes, sleeping and living naked. He also stopped cutting his fingernails and toenails, so that they grew into great curling obstructions. That said, when a risk-taking writer decided to present a manuscript to a respectable publisher as Howard Hughes's authorised (if ghost-written) autobiography, Hughes pulled himself together enough to do a conference call from his hideout which established beyond doubt that the book was a fabrication to which he had contributed nothing, least of all his authorisation or per-mission.

Thereafter, however, his condition deteriorated. He stopped leaving his bedroom and, as he took more and more drugs, even stopped leaving his bed. Food became an irritation, rather than a necessity, and one of the richest men in the world began to slowly starve to death. When it became necessary to leave his location and go elsewhere, the strain of the move killed him and he died on the plane. The post-mortem showed him to be severely emaciated, as well as heavily medicated.

Agoraphobia is one of those rare fears that comes, not in single file, but in battalions. If it simply meant that the sufferer was afraid to go outside their own door, it might be easier to deal with, but, because it is usually entwined with a myriad other fears or ailments, it is one of the hardest phobias to treat or to shake.

The other factor militating against early and effective intervention is that friends and relations become enmeshed in the problem. Rather than helping to solve it, they become enablers, bringing food and other supplies to the person as they isolate themselves from the outside world. This, in turn, contributes to obesity, a complication frequently found with agoraphobia. Although, by its nature, agoraphobia is a hidden and a secret phobia, and therefore produces few famous sufferers (except when the details emerge, posthumously, as they did in the case of Howard Hughes), anecdotal accounts abound of – for example – nurses who gradually restrict themselves to night-work, dealing with comatose patients in their last days. They do their job beautifully. And, since food may be a profound comfort, they become obese. Which, in turn strengthens their allegiance to a job which does not necessitate them meeting people who might comment on their girth.

One of the famous cases of complicated agoraphobia involved morbid obesity. Brian Wilson of the Beach Boys was always regarded by the other members of the band as a bit off-centre, but as the group came to fame during the drug-sodden 1960s, his peculiarities were not seen as particularly exceptional. Wilson was central to the phenomenal success of the Beach Boys. He was producer, arranger, songwriter. He could do lead vocals and backing vocals. He could harmonise in falsetto. All of which helped the Beach Boys to two dozen Top 40 hits.

The early signs of agoraphobia came into view during his wife Marilynn's pregnancy. He put a fridge in their bedroom, so that he could eat in the room, and slept most of the day there, until 'the vibrations' in that room got to him and provoked him into moving to another. After his baby, Carnie, was born, according to Steven Gaines, biographer of the Beach Boys, it got worse: 'Retreating further and further, less and less interested in friends and going out, Brian stayed in bed later into the day, until he finally took to bed altogether. He would stay there for many years.'

It was hard to tell how much of his behaviour was caused by true mental illness, as opposed to fake craziness aimed at keeping the band – which he had come to see as a self-made monster which was eating him alive – away from him. He had periods of deep depression when he became suicidal. On one occasion, he left the house for long enough to dig a grave in his back garden, announcing that he was going to jump off the roof of the house into it.

He spent time in mental hospitals but seemed to make no permanent improvement as a result, mixing prescribed medication with illegal medication so that he was stoned most, if not all of the time. Some of the medication exacerbated his already enormous appetite, so that his weight went over three hundred pounds at one point. When the band and his wife involved a Dr Eugene Landy in his treatment, the latter isolated him from them and attained a Svengali-like influence over him. Landy was later struck off the register of medical practitioners.

When he reached his sixties, Wilson's illnesses came under some kind of control and he recently began to do successful international tours with the Brian Wilson Band.

Other famous sufferers include Kim Basinger, the actor, who maintains that she was so self-conscious about auditions requiring her to strip off to her underwear that she allowed other girls to get the big parts and consequent awards, while she would go home, play the piano and scream her misery out loud. This, she maintains, led to her agoraphobia.

Earlier in this chapter, Dr David V. Sheehan was quoted defining agoraphobia as 'one of the great imposters in medical practice'. It arrives in disguise and puts on a series of other guises, so that it may not be recognised for what it is until the sufferer is actually confined to their own home, suffering from 'agoraphobic syndrome', the symptoms of which may vary in intensity over several years.

'The physician is faced with two major problems in dealing with these patients,' says Sheehan. 'First, the basic anxiety must be controlled. Then the patient must overcome patterns of avoiding specific situations (the agoraphobia and other phobias) that complicate the original anxiety.'

Some of the newer anti-depressants have proven to be more effective than older tranquillisers in controlling the panic attacks associated with agoraphobia, which has led to a belief that this ailment may be the product of a chemical imbalance. Once the panic attacks have been brought under control, the avoidance behaviours the sufferer has put in place to prevent the attacks can be addressed through behaviour therapy techniques, including desensitisation. This is a technique by which the agoraphobic is helped, step by step, to put themselves in situations about which they have been phobic. Each step gives the sufferer a little more confidence, and eventually they may be able to resume a more normal life, possibly with the help of (some) ongoing prescription medication.

14

Fear of Water or Drowning: Aquaphobia

'Stylish Juxtaposition' might have been the name of a Pablo Picasso work, had he ever crossed paths with Ralph Lauren. Somewhere they would never have encountered each other was at a pool party or beach club, for both men had – still has in the case of Mr Lauren – a morbid fear of drowning.

Intense palpitations, teeth-grinding fright and almost fatal anxiety are just some of the symptoms people with aquaphobia will suffer on confronting a body of water. Indeed, in more severe cases, sufferers can't bear to even look at a large bucket or tub of water, let alone toy with the idea of dipping their toe in it – literally.

Aquaphobia – the fear of water – has become a catch-all term to include the more specific fear of drowning. This is not to be confused with hydrophobia, which is in fact a symptom of latter-stage rabies. Hydrophobia's symptoms include a fear of drinking liquids, despite rageing thirst.

Fear of water is not a naturally-occurring human characteristic. Even when people born and raised in deserts first see water, they don't go pale all over and avert their eyes. They just want to know what it is. So when a full-blown case of aquaphobia manifests itself, it's virtually always as a result of a traumatic experience involving water. A near-drowning in the bath as a toddler may leave said toddler with an unhappy but deeply-rooted fear, as can being immersed in water during horseplay.

Some groups quite deliberately segment their view of water. In the days when sailing ships carried passengers and cargo across the oceans, death at sea had to be factored into the thinking of the men who spent most of their lives at sea.

Stories of great and horrible shipwrecks were part of the lore of the sea – like the HMS *Birkenhead*, which was lost in 1845 and was the first ship where women and children were put first into the lifeboats while the sailors stood to attention on the deck in perfect discipline. Up to that point, when a ship started to go down, it was every man, woman and child for themselves, which did tend to put women and babes-in-arm at a certain disadvantage. Once the *Birkenhead* set the standard, that stopped.

'To stand and be still to the Birkenhead drill is a damn tough bullet to chew,' was how Rudyard Kipling summed it up. But sailors lived and died by the Birkenhead drill from that point on. Few of them would have learned to swim. Many if not most sailors in the past deliberately avoided learning to swim, on the principle that if you were washed overboard, your chances of a quick death, as opposed to several days of thirst and exposure before you died, were improved if you couldn't swim.

'The sea's for sailin' boats on, not swimmin' in,' the sailors' view, was a practical decision, not rooted in a phobic response to water, per se.

Of course, the greater your fear of water and of drowning, the more at risk you are of dying by water, whereas the more competent you are in the sea, the better your chances of survival, as Tim Sears, a thirty-one-year old industrial engineer, found when he fell off his cruise ship. At night. After a few drinks. Without anybody noticing. He immediately started swimming and varied his activity between backstroke, breaststroke and dog paddle. That got him through the night hours. Daylight brought fascinating sights, but none of them took the form of a ship.

'Daylight come and me wanna go home,' he hummed to himself to get a laugh out of it.

It was the last laugh for quite a while. The day delivered dehydration and sunburn. The sea delivered cold. After seventeen hours, he saw a ship, hauled off his yellow T-shirt, tore it with his teeth so it would present a bigger expanse, and waved and screamed. The guys on the ship saw him and put a small boat out to collect him. After they had warmed him and given him liquids, his rescuers radioed the ship off which he had fallen, which was now almost five hundred miles away. The conversation seems to have gone along these lines:

'Hi, there. We're the freighter *Eny*. Can we have a word with the captain?'

'Bridge here.'

'Captain, we're a freighter and we have one of your passengers.'

'Sorry?'

'Yep, his name is Tim and he's a bit sunburned. Also eating us out of house and home.'

'How do you have one of my passengers?'

'He fell off the deck.'

'He what?'

'Seventeen hours ago. You hadn't missed him?'

'Nope.'

Not only had the crew not missed him, the pal with whom he'd boarded, who had missed him, just assumed Tim had got lucky with some female passenger and was a bit occupied. It never occurred to his pal – understandably – that Tim was singing 'The Banana Boat Song' to himself in mid-ocean and getting terminally wet.

What Tim had going for him, once he got over the minor bad luck of falling off his own ship unnoticed, was, first and foremost, that he knew how to swim and could vary his approach to swimming so that his muscles got some variety of stress. He was also in good physical shape. He had been a paratrooper and was used to managing risks. He had a religious faith (a strong positive factor in surmounting crises ranging from explosions to air crashes) and a resolute, rather than crudely cheery, attitude.

'If I'm going to get out of this situation,' he thought, 'I need to keep maintaining and be strong and get through it.'

The key factor, however, was his ability to swim. Had he fallen into ice-cold water (as he did) without the ability to swim, he was, frankly, a goner. According to research conducted in the Laboratory or Exercise and Environmental Medicine at the University of Manitoba in Winnipeg, if you land into icy water, surviving the first minute is crucial. Icy water tends to induce 'cold shock' which causes people to gasp and then hyperventilate, which makes them more likely to inhale freezing water. (This is one of the few situations where being fat helps. Hypothermia that sets in within forty minutes in a skinny person can take an hour to affect a more padded person.)

Because so many people have such a terror of water, a man with the wonderful name of Melon Dash set up the Transpersonal Swimming Institute in Berkeley, California in 1983, specifically to teach sufferers of aquaphobia how to swim. An integral part of the course he designed is to educate people in the basic principles of water. One of which is that, all things being equal, if you put a human in water, said human floats. (Assuming enough water, obviously.) Dash uses physics to convince aquaphobes that all they need to do is breathe and use their limbs to paddle themselves to safety. Versions of this training are now available all over the world, including Ireland, and are markedly successful.

Fear of drowning is one thing. Fear of water is related but separate. In extreme cases aquaphobes will not even sit in a garden where there is a small pond. The symptoms they suffer often include high anxiety, dizziness, nausea, trembling, sweating, an unnatural desire to flee and the sense that if they enter the water they will die. Before the sufferer can even contemplate taking swimming lessons it is often advised that they find a partner they can trust to help them on their journey to recovery. Because, unless they plan to take up residence in the Sahara, sooner or later they are likely to encounter a little puddle. Or a river. Or a heavy downpour.

Which leads inevitably to a little speculation. Just as

America has physical ailments (like 'restless legs') that don't seem to afflict many people in Ireland, maybe aquaphobia doesn't affect that many people in this country. Because I have yet to encounter a support group for water phobics. It may be out there but, thus far, it hasn't generated much media coverage.

Which is not to suggest that it doesn't exist in this country, or that people suffering from it cannot be helped by therapy which introduces them gradually to the presence of water, perhaps by taking several trips to the beach, just for a stroll, before the aquaphobe even attempts to get his or her feet wet. Patience is an essential virtue of any friend or therapist helping out a sufferer of aquaphobia. The treatment for aquaphobia places heavy emphasis on having a healthy regard for the water as well as a reasonable and rational attitude towards using it as an amenity.

One fact that aquaphobes out there may not like to hear is that in natural disasters more people die from drowning than any other way. In an extreme hurricane there will be more deaths due to drowning than from getting battered by violent winds. Earthquakes and landslides also cause huge numbers of fatalities by drowning, be it by enveloping a victim in mud or by smashing a dam and flooding a low-lying area. In one American disaster, people in a town were killed by a flow of molasses.

Obviously natural disasters are indiscriminate and suffering anxiety continually, on the basis that a hurricane might come or a tsunami hit, belongs to the irrational end of the range of fears.

For your average non-swimming worrier, a helpful friend and some good swimming lessons should help them to overcome this debilitating phobia. A trend in recent years has been for middle-aged people who can't swim or who swim badly to take intensive lessons over, say, a weekend. The sense of personal freedom gained from such lessons is enormous. If you dread the holidays because the sea or the swimming pool holds nothing but threats, as far as you're concerned, such lessons can do much more than simply release you from fear.

Fear of oil: oleophobia

The chances are that you will go through life, sure that you will never meet another human being who believes themselves to suffer from an aversion to oil or fear of oil so pronounced as to amount to oleophobia.

You're quite likely, on the other hand, to meet an oleophobic material, especially if you own an iPad. The glass Apple uses for the iPad (and the more recent iPhones) is coated with a polymer to which the oil from human skin does not stick. The polymer is oleophobic, which allows it to stay shiny, clean and transparent despite its owner sweeping their fingers across it and tapping its surface hundreds of times each day.

15

Fear of Clowns: Coulrophobia

It took until the 1980s for this one to surface, which is amazing, given how long circuses have been around. And how horrible they are. (Clowns, not circuses.) Now, at this late stage, we have a term for fear of clowns: coulrophobia. It's rooted in Greek words meaning 'stilt-walker' but it means clown phobia.

I've always hated clowns. Always. From the first time I saw one in a big top. The horses were cool, not least because when a horse lets go, every child thinks the volume of waste material and the smell are riotously funny. Plus you realise for the first time that it steams when fresh.

I liked the lions, too, although my mother said they were full of tranquillisers. I think she thought this would reduce a nascent terror I didn't actually have, but it also served to explain why they got up on their platforms and had to be whipped into jumping through a burning hoop. They looked moth-eaten, old and bored. Certainly not scary.

But the clowns! I was terrified that they'd get loose and come at me with their horrible fixed expressions, hard roundy noses and – worst of all – one of them had a baldy wig. You know those yokes that cover the wearer's hair with a vomitous rubbery condom out of the sides of which sprouts hair? Their real forehead wrinkles up and then it meets this obvious unyielding bathing cap. With hair.

'Something about the painted face, the fake smile,' Johnny Depp once remarked, confessing to having this phobia. 'There always seemed to be a darkness lurking just under the surface, a potential for real evil.'

And that's not even to address those long, long shoes. I've

always hated those extra-long shoes. Even if a pair of pumps is otherwise perfect, I won't buy them if they have extra-long toe pieces. When my bank had an advertisement campaign involving a girl dressed up as a bug (why?), wearing extra long pointy-up shoes, I'd have moved my account elsewhere except that elsewhere wouldn't have wanted me.

Think about those extra-long shoes. Just think about them. Think about them from the point of view of a child. Children are smart. They don't find it funny to see a guy with a white face on him and big buttons tramping around in extra-long shoes. They think the thing called Clown should cut off the front of his shoes.

And while I'm at it, you know what you can do with Charlie Chaplin? The birthday parties I attended in my youth where the highlight was the birthday girl's uncle setting up a projector and playing a black-and-white Charlie Chaplin movie. You'd be made to sit down, feeling sick from the awful food they made you eat at birthday parties (cornflake crispies made with cooking chocolate that coated the inside of your mouth with sweet soap scum for a week) and were forced to watch this sinister creep doing things that made no sense and were never, ever funny.

Try it. Download a Charlie Chaplin movie – any Charlie Chaplin movie. Play it for a bunch of children and count the laughs. You won't need one of those clicker counters, because the sum total of the hilarity will amount to none. Then play it for adults. They'll waste a lot of time explaining to each other how much of an artist Chaplin was. Laughs? None. Because why? Because he was not funny. Ever. Now, Harold Lloyd, the guy on the clock, was genuinely funny. But the birthday girl's uncle never had reels of him.(The birthday girl's uncle also had a form of dyslexia which meant that he couldn't get the order of the reels of film right, so you started with the end, then got the beginning and finished off with the middle.) I figure Chaplin just had better spin doctors than the man on the clock. Or else he had damn-all competition at the time.

The key misapprehension about Chaplin, which extends through to clowns, is the adult belief that children are stupid. Nothing else explains the way we – and McDonald's – inflict clowns on them. This is something the Minister for Children needs to address. Because the evidence is in. This is not an impression. This is fact.

A study conducted by the University of Sheffield found that children did not like clown decor in hospital or doctor's office settings. The survey was quite properly conducted in order to find out what they'd like or not like when the hospital was redesigned. Loud and clear, the children made it clear: forget clowns. No clowns, thank you very much. The adults involved may have reeled back in amazement. Well, fancy that. Kids who don't like clowns. Who'd have thought?

'As adults we make assumptions about what works for children,' Dr Penny Curtis, a researcher, stated. 'We found that clowns are universally disliked by children. Some found them quite frightening and unknowable.'

Just what 'unknowable' means is unclear and academic but you get the drift. Clowns=bad.

One of the worst clowns is Ronald McDonald. I know, I know. All those Ronald McDonald houses for the families of sick children are good. But the clown obeys the general rule of clowns=bad. I gave up going to Walmart, before I discovered the full awful truth about them, simply because whenever I was in the States and visited one of their hyper stores, I would turn the corner into the frozen foods section and find myself face to face with a shiny hard life-size Ronald. Put the heart crossways in me, it did.

A friend of mine who is now a famous TV personality once worked as a Ronald McDonald. He was poor at the time. But he was enthralled by the standards applied by McDonald's to the students who got picked to be Ronald. I can't remember if the Gardai did child-protection vetting on them but the selection and training process was comprehensively rigorous, and governed by a hefty manual.

One of the provisions in the manual was that two girls who accompanied Ronald everywhere had to pull him aside every three minutes and spray breath freshener into his mouth. He could be tall, multicoloured, caked in make-up and wearing an unremitting rictus, but his breath had to smell fresh and clean.

Even though coulrophobia is a relatively recent coinage, it's pretty obvious that many film makers and weird geniuses like Stephen King have wanted to explode the clown myth for a long time. Evil clowns have increasingly figured in movies, once Batman started the trend. The only clown in a movie who did what clowns are supposed to do – be pathetic and funny at the same time – was played by Bill Murray in a 1990 film entitled *Quickchange*. Murray's a burned-out crook who decides to do a bank robbery dressed as a clown and the doorman in the bank tries to bar him coming in. The security guy says something like, 'Closing time, Bozo,' and Murray, pulling out a snub-nosed automatic from his voluminous clothes, gestures him to one side with the response 'And that's *Mister* Bozo to you.'

Now, fine, Bill Murray was playing a fictional villain. But one of the worst non-fiction villains, John Wayne Gacy, a Chicago building contractor, used to dress up as Pogo the clown and entertain local children. All together now: 'Aaaah.' Then a young man to whom Gacy had offered a job disappeared and when the police visited his premises, they noticed an odd smell. (Altogether now: 'Ughh.') Said smell emanated from the thirty-three dead bodies secreted beneath the floor boards. He confessed to having picked up, chloroformed, raped and strangled young boys in the 1970s, and was eventually executed in 1994.

John Wayne Gacy, having been convicted of more murders than anybody else in American history, changed the risk level associated with clowns. Think of it this way. Globally, the statistical odds of being killed on a single airline flight are one in 9.2 million. The population of Chicago is 9.5 million. That's where Gacy strangled those thirty-three people. So, between 1972 and 1978, the odds of being strangled by a clown in Chicago were slightly higher than the chances of dying on a plane.

Since then, of course, Gacy's murderous progress was finished by his execution, so the odds of being killed by a clown have greatly reduced. If that's any consolation to someone who suffers from fear of clowns.

By the way, I should mention, while I'm at it, that during the time he was in prison awaiting execution, John Wayne Gacy obsessively painted (or, perhaps more accurately, copied) Disney figures. These paintings were publicly burned by his relatives as soon as he was dead. They released photographs, showing the image of Mickey Mouse being consumed by flames. And a good thing, too. He's another horrible persona inflicted on too many generations of children. Mickey Mouse. As worthless, unfunny and peculiar as any clown, and as durable as plastic.

16

Fear of Fire

Fire is one of humanity's great fears. London's Great Fire of September 1666 was a classic, in that when it started in a bakery, it seemed so minor that the Lord Mayor's view was that 'a woman might piss it out'. (Bakeries have been at the heart of some of history's most disastrous fires because flour is highly flammable. The bakery beside the picturesque windmills in Skerries, in north County Dublin was destroyed by flour-explosion and fire.)

What happened in London was that a strong wind drove the flames in front of it for four days, destroying Old St Paul's Cathedral, eight-seven churches and more than 13,000 houses and public buildings, including the Guildhall, the Custom House, and the Royal Exchange

'The stones of Paul's flew like grenades, the lead mealting downe the streetes in a streame,' wrote John Evelyn in his diary at the time. 'The very pavements of them glowing with fiery rednesse, so as nor horse nor man was able to tread on them.'

Did the city learn? Not really. London had forty further fires in the following hundred and forty years. Those fires did disproportionate damage, too. A writer in the eighteenth century estimated that at least fifty houses ordinarily burned in London for every five lost in Paris, although he didn't offer a good reason.

Other cities including Amsterdam suffered dreadfully, too. In Moscow in 1737 more than two thousand people died in an early-morning fire. Toulouse was all but consumed in 1463, as was Bourges in 1487.

In *Ulysses*, Mr Kernan and the publican Mr Crimmins discuss the news they've just heard of the burning of a paddle steamer called the *General Slocum*, carrying thousands of holidaymakers up New York's East River in June 1904. When fire broke out below decks, the oil tanks exploded, and instead of steering towards the shore, the captain kept the ship going.

When passengers realised the ship was sinking, they grabbed life jackets, only to find they had rotted. They could not get the lifeboats off their rusted stands. The crew had no firefighting training and showed almost uniform cowardice.

'I will never be able to forget the scene, the utter horror of it,' wrote the health commissioner, who happened to be on shore in full sight of the fireball. 'Along the beach the boats were carrying in the living and dying and towing in the dead.'

More than a thousand people had set out that day with high hopes, dressed in holiday finery. Some of the deaths were caused by the finery – women and children drowned when forced overboard because of the weight of their clothing.

Even at a distance of thousands of miles and several days, Joyce's two characters were struck by the 'heartrending scenes' in the newspapers.

'Men trampling down women and children. Most brutal thing. What do they say was the cause? Spontaneous combustion. Most scandalous revelation. Not a single life-boat would float and the fire-hose all burst…and America, they say, is the land of the free.'

Yet, just six years later, another fire, this time on land, came close to the horror of the burning of the *General Slocum*. This was the Triangle Shirtwaist Factory in 1911. Thousands of immigrant girls went to work in the garment district of New York at the beginning of the twentieth century. Young women, mostly Jewish and Italian, worked in the Triangle factory's eighth, ninth and tenth floors in appalling conditions. They were crowded together, sewing highly flammable fabrics with swatches of those fabrics lying on the floor around them and huge baskets of remnants everywhere. The fire doors were locked, lest the girls sneak out to have a cigarette or leave early.

When the fire broke out in the late afternoon of 25 March

– a Saturday – a clever girl on one floor telephoned people on another floor to tell them to get out. Their flight wasn't helped by the actions of a foreman, who held the key to an essential escape door but who fled before unlocking the door.

Within three minutes, the stairs were impassible. A heroic lift operator brought his lift up and down several times, rescuing dozens of girls, but eventually had to stop because the skin of his hands was melting on to the controls. Soon, a sound was heard in the streets of Manhattan that was to be heard again during 9/11: the noise of bodies falling from a great height. The girls, forced out by flames, jumped to their deaths. One man and his girlfriend kissed and jumped together.

One hundred and forty-six people died, all but seventeen of them women. They died as a result of smoke inhalation, burning and falling.

Afterwards, the owners were taken to court, where the case failed because the smart defence attorney worked out that some of the survivors had been coached in their testimony. (Of course they had – terrified young illiterates facing the might of the judicial system.) However, civil cases later succeeded – and major regulations and inspection systems were put in place in New York as a consequence of the Triangle Shirtwaist fire.

Dublin's Stardust fire in 1981 was one of Ireland's worst disasters, taking the lives of teenagers out for a Valentine's Day dance. Some of the survivors still bear physical and psychological scarring. A tiny, beautiful memorial garden in Beaumont Hospital reminds visitors of the Stardust tragedy. It includes a verse from 'For the Fallen', a poem by Laurence Binyon about the young people lost in the First World War:

> They shall not grow old, as we that are left grow old;
> Age shall not weary them, nor the years condemn.
> At the going down of the sun and in the morning;
> We will remember them.

If you're afraid of fire, take precautions. Keep the floor clear of debris. Unplug devices at night. Get a smoke alarm.

17

Fear of Getting Old: Gerontophobia

The first point to make about old age is that, whatever its disadvantages, it beats the alternative. Which is not to downgrade the fear of old age, which has been around for long, long time. These days, when someone pops their clogs in their eighties or nineties, someone at the funeral inevitably comments that the dead one 'had a good innings'. Why cricket should be the analogy of choice is not clear, but it sounds better, somehow, at a funeral, than 'he had a good eighteen holes'.

Back in the days when 'a good innings' meant that the person survived to their forties, a few hardy souls got under the statistical wire and lived to be really old. Some of them did pretty well in their later years. Sophocles, for example, ran into the situation where his sons took him to court to have him declared mentally incompetent, so they could take over the management of his estate. The playwright turned up in court with the manuscript of the play on which he was working at the time and read it aloud in court. The judges decided it definitely wasn't the work an incompetent old man and put the skids under his offspring.

Isocrates, a noted Greek rhetorician, wrote a masterpiece in his mid-nineties. Plato was hard at work up to his death, which happened when he was in his early eighties. Socrates taught himself to play the lyre in his old age. Samuel Johnson lived – by the standards of his time – to the great age of seventy-five and was productive throughout his life. Voltaire was the same. In the twentieth century, Churchill, even pickled, as he usually was, in alcohol, lived to be seriously old and was working long past retirement age. Konrad

Adenauer, the German Chancellor who dragged his country back to prosperity after the Second World War, was pushing seventy when he came to power. In Ireland, the architect of the modern Irish economy, T.K. Whittaker, was still being consulted for his views on the collapsed Irish economy in 2011, when he was ninety-four.

The Roman moralist, Cicero, wrote a book called *De Senectute* (*Of Old Age*), in which he addressed the four negatives then popularly associated with getting older. The first was that age prevented a man from being of public influence. He nailed that with examples. The second was that it 'produced great infirmities of body.' Uh uh, said Cicero. Great infirmities happen in old age only if you've lived like there was no tomorrow. (Tell that to decent-living people in dire need of a hip replacement.) The third drawback of old age, in his time, was that it reduced the ability to enjoy the gratification of the senses, this being Ancient Rome before Viagra. On this one, Cicero had to accept that the sensual passions are not necessarily in overdrive when someone hits their nineties. Ah, but, he says, this releases you to concentrate on other pleasures, such as those of the table and the wine bottle.

He brings the same determined positivity to addressing the last of the four fears of old age: that it brings the older person closer to death. He employs the old hit-by-a-bus theory. You know how some folk reject statistics indicating that their chances of living to a grand old age would be improved if they stopped smoking fifty fags a day, drinking eight pints a night and lying on the couch watching reality TV by saying, 'Sure I could get hit by a bus in the morning'? I've always felt this to be a slur on Bus Eireann and don't understand why they don't put out figures proving that your chances of being hit by one of their buses are considerably smaller than the odds you'll get hit by a car, motorbike or slammed door.

Cicero went the hit-by-bus route, pointing out that young people die all the time, while older people, once they survive to be old, often survive to be older still. Which was statistically true then and is true to this day.

The problem with getting older is not actually getting chronologically older. It's about developing the signs and symptoms of getting older and not liking them. Before Cicero decided to do public relations on behalf of the golden years (as they used to be called, particularly by banks offering copper-bottomed safe investment in the form of bank shares – ah those innocent days of recent yore). Lucian, one of the great Greek poets, got more brutally realistic about the condition.

'The years will wear these charming features; this forehead, time-withered, will be crossed with wrinkles; this beauty will become the prey of the pitiless old age which is creeping up silently, step by step. They will say: "She was beautiful." And you will be utterly wretched; you will say you mirror lies.'

Lucian seems to have believed that old age was a gender-specific affliction centred on women, whereas Chaucer frequently looked at old age as a male problem. One of the yarns in *The Canterbury Tales* concerns a rich old man who marries a gorgeous younger woman. The old man is named January, his bride, May. Not long after their wedding, January catches May in flagrante with a good-looking younger man. May keeps her wits about her, pointing out to her husband that age may have disimproved his eyesight and this disimprovement has led to him seeing things that aren't there at all, at all. January, understandably, doesn't wish to believe his eyes, so he goes along with this explanation, thereby saving his marriage, for what it's worth.

During the Renaissance, an aristocrat from Venice got what we would now describe as a wake-up call from his doctor. Luigi Cornaro was in his thirties when he became seriously ill. He pulled through but his doctor pointed out that if he continued to live as he was living, he would not get much further than his thirties. Cornaro seems to have been the ultimate exception to the statistics that indicate, inter alia, that, even after suffering a heart attack, six out of every seven patients make no enduring dietary or exercise changes.

He sobered up, began to study older people to identify the behaviour that contributed to their survival and eventually produced his magnum opus, *A Treatise of Health and Long Life and the Sure Means of Attaining It.*

'Long life' he defined as a hundred years of age and he set out to get there himself, even if it meant self-deprivation. And it did. He ate an extremely restricted diet, hundreds of years before experiments with rats proved that a rat restricted to considerably fewer than the calories any normal rat would eat was likely to survive much longer than normal. It works for rats. It worked for him, too – he very nearly made it to the century.

More of us would emulate him if we didn't smoke and didn't get fat. What the World Health Organisation calls 'globesity' is now close to competing with cigarettes as the most preventable cause of death.

But restricting his calorie intake wasn't the only apparently modern action Carnaro took. Exercise was high on his agenda, as were stress-busting leisure activities like gardening and getting a good night's sleep.

That last one is becoming more and more difficult to achieve, as long commutes to work and other factors interfere with sleep patterns. Alan Rechtschaffen at the University of Chicago systematically inflicted sleep-deprivation on a group of rats. (It's always rats who are put racing through mazes, shuddering through electric shocks or being starved. We'd never do it to rabbits or dolphins.)

The first way the rats reacted to lack of sleep was to eat more. Anyone who has ever had to work through the night knows that the urge to eat is as constant as the urge to sleep and that eating serves as a way to get more energy. 'Fat and lazy' are two words that really don't belong together, often as they're placed side by side. People can work very hard and become very fat at the same time, if they're using sugar and fat to give them the jolt of energy of which sleep deprivation robs them. Which, of course, puts two dangers together, but let's go back to the unfortunate rats.

Within a week, these rats began to suffer fluctuating body temperatures. Their hair began to fall out. Any injuries they had refused to heal. Within a month, they were all dead. But, I hear you say, those are only rats and anyway, serve them bloody right, having carried the plague all over the world like a medieval and deeply evil version of FedEx.

It turns out that what goes for rats, in terms of sleep deprivation, goes for humans, too. The Harvard Nurses' Health Study monitored 80,000 American nurses over a quarter of a century. It found a strong link between chronic sleep deprivation and increased risk of a range of diseases, including breast cancer, colon cancer, and coronary heart disease. If nurses got, on average, only five hours of sleep a night, they were much more likely to get heart disease than nurses getting six hours sleep a night, and they in turn, were at greater risk than those who slept seven hours a night.

If you watch your weight, take exercise, get the right amount of sleep, work on being optimistic and don't take risks just for the adrenalin rush of taking risks, your chances of living to be old improve. So what are you afraid of?

The answer to that tends to take two very different forms.

The first is a growing fear of ending up demented, in a nursing home, and the bad news here is that, so far, none of the research into Alzheimer's disease has come up with a foolproof preventive method, whether that lie in lifestyle choices or in available pharmaceuticals. The preponderance of evidence suggests that taking exercise, being social and involving yourself in intellectual pursuits might prevent or postpone Alzheimers but it's an unproven suggestion, and while drugs are now available on prescription, they tend to be of use only: a) to people who have already been diagnosed with this form of dementia; and b) in slowing down the progress of the disease, rather than halting it completely. Worrying about it, however, does rather waste the time you're free of it.

The other fear associating with getting older is looking older. Oscar Wilde's *The Portrait of Dorian Gray* is the quintessential exploration of this fear. Dorian has a portrait painted of himself in his youthful prime and expresses the wish that the painting, rather than him, could experience the depredations of passing time.

He gets his wish, staying handsome and unwrinkled despite his dissolute life, while the painting, now hidden in an attic and visited only by its subject, absorbs all the punishment.

'Hour by hour, and week by week, the thing upon the canvas was growing old. It might escape the hideousness of sin, but the hideousness of age was in store for it. The cheeks would become hollow or flaccid. Yellow crow's feet would creep around the fading eyes and make them horrible. The hair would lose its brightness, the mouth would gape or droop, would be foolish or gross, as the mouths of old men are. There would be the wrinkled throat, the cold, blue-veined hands, the twisted body...'

Now, anybody with a titter of wit would have said to Dorian: 'Undo the spell. Unwish your wish. Dammit to hell, my man, what's wrong with growing old gracefully? Stiffen your spine, there, my boy, and get over this vainglorious hatred you have of looking old. It is only natural.'

Of course it is 'only natural'. But what is natural is not necessarily welcome. It was Shakespeare in his middle age, who wrote the speech in *As You Like It* about the seven ages his character, Jaques, believed that men live through. It was not warm and fuzzy about old age:

> *The sixth age shifts*
> *Into the lean and slipper'd pantaloon,*
> *With spectacles on nose, and pouch on side,*
> *His youthful hose well sav'd, a world too wide,*
> *For his shrunk shank, and his big manly voice,*

Turning again towards childish treble, pipes
And whistles in his sound. Last scene of all,
That ends this strange eventful history,
Is second childishness and mere oblivion,
Sans teeth, sans eyes, sans taste, sans everything.

Long before he was in the 'sans everything' stage, Dorian Gray projected this deterioration on to the portrait and it worked out pretty well until he died. His servants found a raddled, withered horror of a corpse lying beneath the portrait of their master as a handsome young man.

The same kind of theme was taken on by H. Rider Haggard in a novel called *She*, about a woman called Ayesha who has ruled a kingdom in Africa for more than two thousand years, having stepped, as a girl, into a flame of eternal youth. When she falls in love with a young Englishman, she takes him to the flame because she wants him to avoid the exigencies of his best-before date. By way of jollying him into the burn, she steps back into it herself, which is a pity, because it reverses the process.

'Smaller and smaller she grew, and smaller yet, till she was no larger than a monkey,' wrote Rider Haggard. 'Now the skin had puckered into a million wrinkles, and on her shapeless face was the stamp of unutterable age.'

She then, the poor sausage – and I know you're way ahead of me, here – dies. Having given her English fiancé, one imagines, a pretty tough day and a lifelong fear of fire.

Life would have been simpler for Dorian Gray and Ayesha if cosmetic surgery had been available in their time. It was only beginning in Dorian's time, and stories of early disasters demonstrate the terrible risks women (because it was almost exclusively women who availed of cosmetic surgery in the early days) were prepared to take in order to remove, not age, but some of the less pleasing signs of age. (I refer you to the quotes above.) Today, cosmetic surgery is a massive global business, and almost any procedure available around the world is available in Ireland, whether that's a face lift or a thigh lift, an arm lift or a breast lift.

If you want to know more about the details and costs of many of the most popular cosmetic surgical interventions designed to remove signs of ageing, buy my *Mirror, Mirror, Confessions of a Plastic Surgery Addict*. It's an account of how, fifteen years ago, I started a love affair with cosmetic surgery which would continue to this day except that right now I'm too broke to afford the thigh lift I lust after. When I win the Lottery, though…

When I wrote the book about plastic surgery, my son predicted that our business would fold as a result of this public revelation. We would be disgraced and no client would ever come to us again. Other than a couple of (male) clients who said their wives had told them to take a long searching look at me to see if they could spot the scars (they couldn't) it had no outcomes at all. Except that I lost some of the jowly wrinkly bits for a while. The end result of good cosmetic surgery is that one looks less tired, not that one looks artificially young.

However, even though we in Ireland are huge consumers of cosmetic surgery, it tends to evoke one of the country's great sanctimonies. Whenever anyone asks me about it on radio or TV, the vote in the studio and the texts from the home audience invariably agree that cosmetic surgery is the resort of the pathologically vain and the psychologically troubled who have more money than sense and that no decent person would be caught with a face lift. Next day, of course, is when I get the tsunami of covert phone calls, emails and snail mail asking for the address of a good plastic surgeon.

The programme presenters (usually female, average age twenty-eight, untroubled by notions of mortality or the very possibility of ever being old) reproach you virtuously if you've had a bit of facial panel-beating, on the basis that if you were secure in yourself wouldn't you welcome the natural signs of ageing. After all, they say, haven't you earned the wrinkles you have? To which the answer is 'Yeah, same as I earned the smashed brake-light on the car where I introduced it too enthusiastically to a skip, but if I keep the damage as a manifestation of my personal authenticity, you know what? It'll fail the NCT.'

They also seem to have missed the point that not many of us compliment someone else by saying, 'Hey, cute wrinkles!' Doesn't happen. Nor do people rush up to each other trilling, 'Gosh, you look great – you look so old.' Nor does anyone say to an older friend, 'Lordy, those little drawstring lines around your mouth are so pretty.'

The myth of growing old gracefully comes from the imperative of decently desexualising our elders. Every generation has a fundamental need to believe: a) that their parents did sex infrequently and under duress (although the cause of duress is kind of vague); b) that they stopped it at thirty; c) that even when they were at it, they never went beyond the plain vanilla kind. Nobody wants a sexually active granny around – that's why God gave them wrinkly cleavages.

Younger people like older people to conform to stereotype. To be smart but not fashionable. They don't want them confined to the house but they'd like them to leave the house only for comfortably communal activities like delivering meals on wheels. And the problem, at the moment, is that older people have lost all sense of responsibility. They'll get spare skin taken off their faces just as quickly as they'll get their hair cut when it gets too long.

If you share their fear of looking old and have decided to do something surgical about it, a couple of health and safety warnings are in order.

First of all, surgery, by its nature, has risks. Surgery which attracts a preponderance of older people as clientèle (although this is changing) has very particular risks: a general anaesthetic for a forty-year-old has demonstrable hazards attached to it but not such predictable perils as for an eighty-year-old. And eighty year olds, these days, have face lifts.

Secondly, good surgeons are like Volvos: very safe if they're kept serviced. The difference is that surgeons don't have self-diagnostic systems which announce to their users when some of their competences begin to fail. The history of surgery includes a few notable examples of men who went from super-competence to complete incompetence as they developed Alzheimers, their behaviours in the operating theatre mystifying their colleagues and endangering their patients.

No system is in place anywhere to alert patients to diminishing skills on the part of a surgeon. Nor does it require something as major as senile dementia to erode surgical competence, as I found out a couple of years ago. During a consultation before a procedure with one surgeon who'd already worked on my face, I asked a question that wasn't answered. It wasn't an important question and there seemed no discourtesy in the surgeon's moving on to some other issue. But when he paused for breath, the nurse who was present said, 'Terry's anxious about X.' In effect, she re-asked my question. The surgeon gave an immediate and complete answer. After he was gone, the nurse winked at me.

'Goin' a little deaf,' she announced. 'But not ready to wear a hearing aid, just yet. Don' you worry, hon, I'll look out for you.'

I reread the informed consent form in a new light. It told me that because of any number of naturally occurring and unpredictable complications of any kind of surgery, I might die, have a disabling stroke, be grievously unhappy with the end results of the surgery or develop post-operative infection. It didn't tell me that the surgeon, because of a touch of vanity, might not hear the anaesthetist trying to draw his attention to the fact that my vital signs were disimproving. Had this particular smart nurse not been a member of the surgical team, and had I not noticed my question not being answered, I would have signed a form testifying to my understanding of something I couldn't fully have understood, but which would have – in the event of a bad outcome – precluded me from suing the surgeon, assuming I survived. Informed consent? Yeah, right.

Informed consent is one of those concepts whose perceived value greatly outweighs the reality. Particularly, but not exclusively, for cosmetic surgery. The drill is that before you go under the knife, or, if it's liposuction, under the cannula, you're handed a clipboard with as many as ten pages. Most of the ten pages are filled with negative possibilities. However, of necessity, they are general negative possibilities: bad stuff that might happen to anyone undergoing this procedure, anywhere at any time. They do not address the competence, basic, referred or developing, of the specific surgeon.

Basic competence is validated, in the United States, by being 'board-certified'. Many medics with no plastic surgery training are now doing procedures for which they are not board-certified, but the informed consent form never says 'And have you checked that the surgeon you're about to trust – with your face and your life – has been certified for the task?'

The situation in Ireland is even worse, as evidenced by high-profile court cases in the last few years. Those court cases involved quite young women, several of whom were left disfigured and at least one of whom became deadly ill, as a result of the 'cut and fly' routine whereby foreign surgeons fly into Ireland, perform a few dozen surgeries, including breast lifts and face lifts, and fly to their home country immediately thereafter, leaving the aftercare to nurses belonging to the private clinic involved, or in some cases to nobody at all, so the patient ends up taking their problem to an A&E.

If you're thinking about cosmetic surgery, don't go with any clinic that offers a discount if you can pitch up with your wrinkles and your credit card within the next two or three weeks: they're trying to crowd you into consent, lest you go away and have second thoughts. Don't go with any clinic where the consultation lasts a few minutes with a non-medical staffer who is essentially a salesperson. And don't be misled by luxurious reception rooms. It's not the reception rooms that matter. It's the standard of equipment and of skill in the operating theatre. When in doubt, walk away.

Oscar Wilde said that the tragedy of old age is not that one is old, but that one is young. Plastic surgery offers an expensive way to postpone or correct some of the less attractive outward and visible signs of ageing.

Some of the non-surgical procedures now available are less expensive and increasingly effective. As one plastic surgeon told me in 2011, a propos the effect on his business of the downturn in the economy, 'Face lifts are down but Botox and fillers are up.'

Botox and fillers are injected without general anaesthetic. Botox is a derivative of botulism, a form of lethal poisoning. It paralyses some of the muscles that, for example, raise your forehead and create corrugated wrinkles in it. I have it done every six months, because it delivers three improvements to my life. The first is that it prevents me having a forehead like a ploughed field. The second is that it prevents migraine headaches and the pre-headache aura or visual distortion that makes it impossible to drive, read or hold a conversation. (The fact that Botox seems to interrupt the circuit that causes migraines is an accidental but widely observed spin-off of the treatment.) The third is that people I work with don't get scared of me. Before Botox, if I frowned, staff cowered in corners and whimpered softly. For several months after a Botox jab, I can't frown at all. Makes for much better workplace relationships.

18

Fear of Death: Thanataphobia

The shrimp in the move *Shark Tale* sums it all up. It is part of a cocktail about to be eaten by two sharks dining together. A live shrimp cocktail. But this particular shrimp is not going to go gently into that dark bite. When it gets picked as first mouthful, it fights back.

'My sister had a baby and I took it on because she passed away and the baby lost its legs and arms but it's growing and it's fairly happy. I've been working a second shift at the factory to put food on the table but all the love that I see on that little guy's face makes it worth it in the end. True story. Have mercy!'

The shark gets sorry for the pop-eyed shrimp and sets him and the rest of the cocktail free. All together now; 'Aaah.'

Except that, for the shrimp, it's a temporary reprieve. Sooner or later that crustacean is going to die. Same as the rest of us. It's the one eternal verity, the one ineluctable experience. For every species. (Including the cockroach, although he gives it a good run.) Nobody escapes it. Everybody's afraid of it. Indeed, some psychiatrists have suggested that most of what we do in life we do as a way of distracting ourselves from becoming fixated on the terror of death. Not many of us are 'half in love with easeful death', as Keats said he was.

According to Karen Armstrong, an expert on comparative religions, 'It could be argued that every culture, every myth, every religion is founded on profound anxiety about essentially practical problems, which cannot be assuaged by purely logical arguments. The Neanderthals who prepared their dead companion for a new life were, perhaps, engaged in the same game of spiritual make-believe that is common to all myth makers.'

In their wanderings, Boswell and Johnson came to much the same conclusion, with Boswell recording their exchange in his *Life of Johnson*:

'Boswell: But is not the fear of death natural to man?

Johnson: So much so, Sir, that the whole of life is but keeping away the thoughts of it...'

Robert Kastenbaum and Ruth Aisenberg, in their book *The Psychology of Death*, agree.

'There lurks somewhere within us, ready for arousal,' they maintain, 'a complex of attitudes and anxieties based on the realisation that any hour of any day could be doomsday.'

No matter how busy we keep ourselves, the thoughts of death never go away and, down the centuries, have given rise to countless myths and legends concerning the figure crime writer John D. MacDonald dubbed 'the Green Ripper'. One of the myths about death fascinated two very different writers, John O'Hara and Somerset Maugham, each of whom used it, O'Hara as the title of one of his novels. The myth concerns a Turkish merchant whose servant comes back from the local market in a panic. While he was there, he tells the merchant, he spotted Death in the crowd and Death made a hostile gesture to him. He begs the merchant's permission to take his best horse so he can get to Samara, as far away from Death as possible in as short a time as possible. The merchant agrees but out of curiosity, after the servant has ridden off, wanders down to the marketplace himself. Sure enough, he encounters Death there. The merchant, being made of sterner stuff than the servant, approaches Death and asks why Death made the hostile gesture to the servant.

'I made no hostile gesture,' Death responds. 'I suppose I started with surprise at seeing him here, because I have an appointment with him tonight, in Samara.'

Even if they didn't personify death in this way, earlier generations were on better terms with him. Death happened to more people at a younger age in times past and tended to occur at home. As children, my mother and her siblings would visit homes where someone had died and ask to pray at the bedside. Sometimes they actually prayed but most of the time, they had a good gawk at the corpse, and on a few occasions, rigged things so that if the bed was touched, the corpse would suddenly sit up, thereby scaring silly the next visitors. Her generation was not disrespectful to death but they were familiar with it in a way current generations are not.

Even earlier, John Donne, the poet, sat for a portrait wearing grave clothes, including a shroud that came around his chin, as it would to hold up the jaw of a dead person, and knotted at the top of his head in a flowery bow. This most vibrant and sensual of poets ('O, my America, my new found land...') went to considerable trouble to look good and dead for the painter long before he was good and really dead. It seems to have been a boy scout form of preparation for the inevitable. Not unlike the uniform the Holy Faith sisters used to wear when I attended one of their schools. It had a hard white frame over which their veil was pinned. A sister from another order recently explained to me that the structure was meant to look like – and feel like – a coffin, to remind its wearer of their mortality.

Any kind of spiritual make-believe in some way derives from the hope that the religion by which we choose to live or the mythology by which we choose to understand the world around us will, in some way, help us to withstand or surmount death.

Religious people tend to be somewhat less fearful of dying, believing that their soul will survive the destruction of their body.

One man expended much energy seeking to prove, not only that humans have a soul, but that the soul has a weight. It weighs about the same as the average thumb, according to research carried out by a Massachusetts-based surgeon named Duncan Macdougall. Although Macdougall didn't work in the local Consumptives' Home, where people suffering from tuberculosis were cared for, he nonetheless persuaded several of the patients there to go along with an experiment he wanted to conduct. As they neared death, he wanted to put them in a sling which had already been weighed, suspended over an exquisitely subtle weighing scales. That way, when they actually died, he could check if their weight changed. History doesn't record how he pitched this to the consumptives, but at least half a dozen went along with the idea, possibly because they were so sick at that point that they didn't much care.

'A consumptive dying after a long illness wasting his energies, dies with scarcely a movement,' Macdougall noted. 'Their bodies are also very light, and we can be forewarned for hours that a consumptive is dying.'

Nothing like a detached view, when you're doing scientific experiments.

If the beam of the weighing scales, according to Macdougall's theory, demonstrated that the consumptive became lighter at the point of death, which would establish that something had left the body right there and then, and since anything physical the patient might shed (let's not explore this further) would be captured within the sling, a weight change could be explained only by the departure of their soul. You with me? Of course you are.

The first patient was duly loaded into the sling and watched for almost four hours as he approached death.

'Suddenly, coincident with death,' Macdougall recorded, 'the beam end dropped with an audible stroke, hitting against the lower limiting bar and remaining there with no rebound. The loss was ascertained to be three-fourths of an ounce.'

The results of this bizarre death-related study were published in *American Medicine*. For purposes of comparison, dogs were weighed at the point of death. Unlike the TB sufferers, the dogs weren't asked for their permission. They were just sacrificed, yielding up only negative information on the scales: they weighed the same after death as they did in life, which of course, if you're of the Macdougall line of thought, makes perfects sense, since dogs don't have souls and therefore wouldn't lose them (and their putative weight) as they were departing for the canine hereafter.

The whole thing does suggest either that Macdougall was not the full shilling, or that he was fascinated by death and found a way to hang around fresh corpses without actually getting into necrophilia. Today, contact with corpses is minimal and even the brief sight of a dead person is strange, because they are so cosmetised as to be virtually unrecognisable. Hospital staff have to deal, every day, with relatives of terminally ill or extraordinarily aged patients who project their own fear of death on to the patient and demand that everything possible and several things that are impossible be done to keep them alive.

A quite different approach – what you might call the immersion approach – was recommended to followers by Buddhist teacher Thich Nhat Hanh:

'Meditate on the decomposition of the body, how the body bloats and turns violet, how it is eaten by worms until only bits of blood and flesh still cling to the bones, meditate up to the point where only white bones remain, which in turn are slowly worn away and turn into dust.

'Meditate like that, knowing that your own body will undergo the same process.

'Meditate on the corpse until you are calm and at peace, until your mind and heart are light and tranquil and a smile appears on your face. Thus, by overcoming revulsion and fear, life will be seen as infinitely precious, every second of it worth living.'

Bet that put a spring in your step…

In the twentieth and twenty-first centuries, death was demoted to a status little more than a regrettable accident, whereas paintings of the last stages of terminal illness in Victorian times are peacefully beautiful, as if all present were waiting for a rite of passage which was as inevitable and welcome as sleep. Patients were told to 'put their papers in order' if they had a fatal disease, and went home to die among those who loved them.

In that situation, some of those about to die saluted death almost as a friend. On 21 April 1910, a scrap of paper was found by the deathbed of Mark Twain, indicating that up to the moment of embracing the Grim Reaper, Twain had been thinking reasonably positive thoughts about him. (Or her, although I can't see any woman wearing that hooded cloak. Not even on a fat day.)

'Death, the only immortal,' read the note, 'whose peace and refuge are for all. The soiled and the pure, the rich and the poor, the loved and the unloved.'

Which is a lot more philosophical than the thoughts most writers dream up on their deathbeds. Oscar Wilde announced that the wallpaper in his room had to go or he would (and promptly did). Eugene O'Neill, in the Boston Sheraton, whispered, 'I knew it. I knew it. Born in a hotel room and god-dam it, died in a hotel room.'

While we're on the topic of what famous people said as they were about to die, have you noticed that nobody seems to have had a good word to say on a deathbed since the early part of the last century? Now that most of the population dies in hospital, intubated at every available point, their vital signs displayed on green-lit screens to their right and left, few of them say anything much in their last days. Not even 'Mother!' which was always the last word of soldiers dying in battle.

That's a pity, because the one thing most deathbed statements establish is that the person who was centre stage or centre bed at the time seems not to have been as fearful of death as most of them would naturally have been earlier in their lives. Thomas Hobbes, who died of a stroke, murmured that he was about to take his last voyage: 'a great leap in the dark.' When Robert Browning asked his sick wife Elizabeth how she felt, the poet's answer, 'Beautiful' came just before she passed away. Jane Austen, asked if she wanted anything, tranquilly replied 'Nothing but death.' And short story writer

O. Henry (William Sydney Porter) said simply, 'Turn up the lights. I don't want to go home in the dark.'

The ideal death? Most people would choose to die in their sleep. But the widow of an Irish-American photographer named Bill Biggart, who died on 9/11, takes a different view. Biggart was a notorious risk-taker. He had been beaten up by the police in Northern Ireland for getting too close to a demonstration. But he refused to learn, so the final frame of the 150 digital photographs he took in the chaos of Manhattan that day carries an electronic timing indicating that it was snapped six seconds before the second tower collapsed on the photographer.

'He loved crowds,' says his widow, Wendy Doremus. 'He loved the crossfire. The only thing you can say is: if you gotta go, you might as well go doing what you love the most.'

19

Fear of Being Buried Alive

Edgar Allan Poe thought being buried alive was 'too entirely horrible for the purposes of legitimate fiction'. It didn't stop him writing one of the most scary of his short stories, 'The Premature Burial': 'The unendurable oppression of the lungs, the stifling fumes of the damp earth, the clinging to the death garments, the rigid embrace of the narrow house, the blackness of the absolute night, the silence like a sea that overwhelms, the unseen but palpable presence of the conqueror worm,' his narrator imagines, tapping into a fear which is one of humanity's oldest.

For example, Pliny the Elder, in the first century AD, told the story of Acilius, a consul, who, having died, as those around him believed, was placed on his funeral pyre, only to come screamingly alive when the flames engulfed him. By the time the mourners managed to douse the fire, the unfortunate man was well and truly dead.

In the middle ages, several well-known figures were believed to have had premature burial inflicted on them, including the scholar Johannes Duns Scotus. After his 'death' he was placed in a vault, but when it was later opened, he was found in a contorted position inside, his hands torn from trying to get out. Much the same is believed to have happened to Thomas à Kempis, also in the fourteenth century. His exhumed corpse is alleged to have been found with splinters from the lid of his coffin driven into his fingernails, which might have been assumed to evoke only sympathy, but which is believed to have caused the powers-that-were to abandon plans to canonise him, their rationale being that nobody worth making into a saint would have been so conspicuously unwilling to meet his maker.

A century later, a woman named Ann Green, taken down after her hanging, was seen to be still breathing. The executioner tried to rectify his failure by stamping on her but managed, instead, to bring her fully back to life. Justice having been half-done, she was freed and went on to marry and have children.

Stories of sentient entombment surface in almost every era and many have the flavour of a modern urban legend: the essential horrific details are much the same but the location, age, gender and nobility of the victim varies, depending on the purveyor of the parable. One of them, which recurs in different forms, concerned an English Countess, Emma of Edgcumbe, who was stricken by a mysterious illness and, her death certified by their physician, buried by her grieving family in the grounds of their mansion, back when this was permitted. The family retreated roughly a kilometre to the house to grieve and perhaps have a bite to eat. Darkness fell.

Meanwhile, the caretaker visited the new grave with evil intent. He had observed that the Countess, in her coffin, had been wearing some expensive jewellery, and had resolved to relieve her of it at the first opportunity. He went to work with a handy shovel, removing the soil that had been loaded on to the top of the coffin and in due course freed up and opened the lid. The icy winter air revived the countess, who apparently hadn't been dead at all, and she sat up. (Other versions of the story have her wakening due to pain caused when the workman pulled hard on a ring he wished to steal from her finger.) The caretaker threw his spade away and ran as if death itself was in pursuit of him, which may have surprised the Countess, who up to that point had as good a working relationship with her employees as any employer had. He did, however, leave his lantern behind him.

The Countess climbed out of the coffin unaided and, carrying the abandoned lantern, walked through the grounds to the bright windows of her home, where she knocked on the glass. The mourning family inside at first thought they had imagined the sound, but when it recurred, her widower (as he thought he then was) rose up, pulled back the curtain and saw his wife's pale and shadowy form. Understandably, he dropped the curtain and went to the sideboard in search of a quick shot of something strong, to help him get over seeing her ghost. Understandably, nobody else was eager to follow his example when the knocking resumed, but eventually, when the knocking took on an impatient pace that spoke of irritated wife, rather than eerie spectre, the husband went back, had a good look at her and worked up the courage to open the French window and let her in. The conversation between the two can be imagined, starting with her demanding to know why he left her freezing her ass off outside when she'd already had the day from hell.

The countess lived for four decades thereafter, according to legend, but the account of her experience played into an existing terror of being buried alive, which led creative entrepreneurs to come up with, and patent, devices like the sturdy pipe designed to come up from the lid of the coffin, through the soil on top, and stand at about knee height above the grave. While the main purpose of the pipe was to allow the corpse in the coffin to breathe freely when it decided not to be a corpse any more, that wasn't the end of the benefits it offered. The entombed one could whistle or shout up through it, and, in addition it was fitted with a wire which was attached to a flag and a bell. If tugged upon from within the coffin, this wire would cause the flag to unfurl and the bell to ring, prompting immediate rescue by visitors to the grave.

The French went even further and in a different direction. They figured out that the one thing that would prevent premature burial was putrefaction. If the body was good and rotten, that in itself was a guarantee that its owner was good and dead. So they invented what was called the waiting mortuary – and very fetching it was, too.

The waiting mortuary relied heavily on tanks of disinfectant and foliage. The corpse was laid out above a tank of disinfectant, which served a dual purpose. It masked the smell of decay in much the same way as those horrible room sprays mask the smell in modern bathrooms. It also caught any liquids dripping from the corpse. The bodies in these waiting mortuaries were surrounded by foliage so that visiting mourners would not be offended by the sight of the tanks, and the deceased person stayed put until they were so past tense that keeping them for any longer would have amounted to cruel and unusual punishment for the undertakers. Elaborate systems of pulleys attached to dead fingers allowed the corpse to call for help if they found themselves alive in this situation.

So real was the fear of premature burial that these waiting mortuaries became extremely popular, although, oddly, it was the Germans, not the French, their inventors, who turned the concept into a big business, opening the first in Weimar in 1791. At one point, Munich alone had eight of them. However, as time elapsed and not a single corpse stored in them came back to life, their numbers reduced. Or, to put it another way, they died off.

The fear, however, never went away, despite the fact that doctors always sneered at the possibility of premature burial, dismissing noises emanating from coffins during burial as gases escaping from the bodies inside them. That didn't stop individuals – including writer Wilkie Collins, the man credited with inventing the detective story with his novel *The Woman in White* – from setting down in their wills elaborate preventive measures to be undertaken by the executors. One wealthy man went further, leaving one hundred thousand pounds to a friend on condition that the friend, before his benefactor was consigned to the earth, operated on the body to remove the heart and other organs. The man writing the will obviously figured either that his pal might be incentivised to prevent his premature burial, or that the operation of scalpels on him would assuredly wake him up if he was only in a deep sleep at the time.

Terror of premature burial peaked in Victorian times, and with it the black humour with which each era copes with its worst fears, as one limerick from the times illustrates:

There was a young man from Nunhead
Who awoke in his coffin of lead
'It was cosy enough,'
He remarked in a huff,
'But I wasn't aware I was dead.'

As time went on and medicine advanced, fear of premature burial reduced somewhat, but has not disappeared, partly because the horrible possibility has come to pass. In some countries, within some religions, burial alive is regarded as an acceptable punishment, but this possibility is not what keeps the fear of premature burial at the back of the mind. Every time the fear recedes, another report is published of an accidental burial of a live person. On St Stephen's Day in 2010, for example, an eighty-eight-year-old named Maria das Dores de Conceicao was declared dead in the city hospital in Ipatinga, Minas Gerais, in eastern Brazil. She was rushed back to intensive care – coffin and all – when mortuary workers noticed her breathing and stirring. Her granddaughter later said that her grandmother looked very much alive when she saw her in the hospital and added that the family were going to sue over the disrespect shown the old lady.

In June 2011, a woman in Russia 'died' unexpectedly of a heart attack in her forty-ninth year. Fagilyu Muhametzyanov woke up to find herself in a coffin, surrounded by weeping relatives. She screamed the place down and was immediately taken back to hospital, where – sadly – she died within minutes of a second heart attack.

One other premature burial in 2011 was self-induced and didn't involve a coffin. Seventeen year old Matt Mina dug a deep hole on Newport Beach in California. A really deep hole. More a tunnel, really. But six feet deep, anyway – Matt was an energetic lad.

Then the walls of his excavation fell in on him and he was buried alive. He managed to create a pocket of air by compressing the sand around his face, and shouted loudly enough to be heard by people on the beach above. The emergency services were immediately called, and holidaymakers got to work digging out the sand before they arrived.

'He's moving,' someone yelled when the digging was half-way through, and some bright spark cut a hole in a rubber bucket (to allow him to breathe) before putting it over his head (to prevent fresh sand from falling into his mouth.) After forty minutes, Matt was on his way to hospital, alive, if somewhat shaken by the experience.

And – just in case you are one of the people with a morbid fear of being buried alive – do not persuade yourself that you can make it a condition of inheritance that those you love disembowel you before they bury you. We have laws about interfering with corpses that undoubtedly include organ removal, even if the objective is resuscitation.

20

Fear of the Undead

Between 2005 and 2009, the Royal Irish Academy funded an archaeological project on a site overlooking Lough Key at Kilteasheen, Knockvicar, County Roscommon. The project has already figured in a Channel 5 documentary and will be included in *National Geographic* in 2012.

The scale of the project is impressive. Three thousand skeletons were buried in the area over a few centuries, often directly on top of one another. But what's fascinating is that two of the skeletons, that of a young man and an older man, found lying side by side, had rocks jammed into their mouths with enormous force.

'One of them was lying with his head looking straight up, and a large black stone had been deliberately thrust into his mouth,' says Chris Read, head of Applied Archaeology at IT Sligo. 'The other had his head turned to the side and had an even larger stone wedged violently into his mouth so that his jaws were almost dislocated.'

The two men were buried in this way around 1300 years ago to prevent them rising from their graves to wander the earth as 'revenants', in much the same way as cultures that believe in vampires specialised in burials involving stakes through the heart to prevent the individuals from becoming the undead.

The burials in Roscommon predate the arrival of vampires in European culture, but apparently Irish communities at the time believed that revenants or ghosts could come back to haunt those who had done them no favours while they were alive. In fact, the theory is that Bram Stoker was inspired to write *Dracula*, not by Romanian legends, but by an Irish folk tale about a chieftain who wouldn't stay dead and was always on the lookout for a bowl of fresh blood to keep him going.

Why Stoker would have ignored the well-established European fascination with vampirism is difficult to compute. As early as 1591, in Breslau, rumours circulated about a shoemaker who, having died by suicide, was believed to visit people in their beds and give them a good squeeze. This was unwelcome to the locals, and – more than six months after his death – they dug him up to check on him and decided that he bore definite signs of vampirism. Nothing to be done but drive a stake through the heart. No doubt the shoemaker's corpse groaned as this happened. Vampires always emitted a satisfying moan as they became stakeholders.

'Many of the so-called signs of a vampire will be recognised as natural post-mortem phenomena: growth of hair and nails; the peeling off of the upper layer of skin to expose a 'new' skin underneath, whose red colour was taken as proof of ingestion of blood from living victims,' writes Robert Wilkins. 'The pressure of gasses formed as a consequence of putrefaction can adequately explain a variety of vampire signs – the erection, the oozing of blood from the mouth, the bloated, well-fed appearance of some of the corpses. The groan of the vampire as he was staked through the heart was due to the forcible expulsion of gas from the chest cavity out through the mouth.'

On the other side of the world, the big fear of the undead focused on the zombie, a dead person reanimated by magic. The marvellous African-American novelist and folklorist Zora Neale Hurston, researching zombies in the 1930s in Haiti, came across people who so passionately believed they had seen dead people that she came to the conclusion that the zombie delusion might have resulted from recreational drugs taken as part of the funeral rites.

'What is more,' she added, 'if science ever gets to the bottom of voodoo in Haiti and Africa, it will be found that some important medical secrets, still unknown to medical science, give it its power.'

An alternative explanation of the survival of zombies in popular culture is that they make for great terror figures in horror movies.

Ghosts, of course, are always with us. Except in modern houses (where the odd poltergeist fills the gap for the bored). Old houses have dry-rot, woodworm, spiders' webs – and ghosts for the gullible. Some of the most intelligent people around believe in them and have always believed in them. Arthur Conan Doyle, the doctor who created the fictive master of logic and ruthless observation, Sherlock Holmes, bought spiritualism, hook, line and sinker. The most amateurish fakery fooled him into thinking that he had seen a real live (or, more probably, a real dead) ghost. It never seemed to occur to him that it was a bit strange that ghosts returning from what we assume is a better and more enlightened life, were a shed-load less interesting than they'd been when alive. The level of banality communicated by most ghosts is astonishing. Except, of course, where chicanery is deployed, as callers to RTÉ's *Liveline* in the autumn of 2011 suggested had happened when a spiritualist seemed to be receiving a feed of information on members of the audience from an individual in the light box at the back of the theatre. Some of those who chose to talk to Joe on the topic were genuinely grieved by the possibility that they'd been the victims of trickery. They desperately wanted to believe that their granny could be spectrally summoned on to the stage by the spiritualist and would send them a comforting message from beyond.

Ghosts you either believe in, suspending your rational brain like Conan Doyle, or you don't. If you're not convinced about them, you see them as being a bit like the gas created by the rotting of a corpse: derived from natural processes but conflated by circumstances into packing more supernatural significance than they're entitled to. People in a heightened emotional state have been known to interpret the creaking of old furniture combined with the movement of a curtain as a very definite ghost. (And if you ever want a ghost story that will make your children laugh, rather than get nightmares, get hold of 'The Canterville Ghost', which proves that Oscar Wilde could out-Dahl Roald Dahl.)

My parents managed to be utterly cynical about ghosts as a concept, while firmly believing they had witnessed a ghost themselves. When they were newly-weds, they rented a vast old house in Tallaght, which was then a place of fields and streams and wooded copses. The house had no electricity. One night, my father blew out the candle and the two of them were well on the way to sleep when someone walked across the room.

'Did you hear that?' my mother asked.

My father, sitting up in bed and striking a match, said he had. He searched the room by candlelight. Nothing. He was about to blow out the candle when my mother indicated that this was one night on which she wanted illuminated sleep, so he left it unsnuffed. About ten minutes later, the footsteps walked back. The two of them were mystified, because, although the footsteps went towards a door on that occasion, they came from a wall.

The following day, my mother went to the lodge at the end of the driveway leading to the big house to talk to the woman who had lived there for decades. Oh, yeah, the woman said, making tea and taking biscuits out of a tin. The ghost.

The ghost, apparently, was one of a pair of brothers, the sons of the family who had once owned the house. The brothers had fallen out over their parents' will and one of them had killed the other in a nearby water mill. He had eventually been charged with the murder, convicted and hanged but still walked from the house to the mill as a ghost, his soul uneased by the execution of his body.

My mother wanted to know why he walked through a wall. This, the neighbour explained, was because that particular wall concealed the entrance to a tunnel leading from the house to the old mill. That night, after my father cycled home from work, the two of them stripped the wallpaper off the relevant wall and broke open the door that had been plastered into place behind it. They explored the tunnel with the fearlessness of youth and eventually used it as a place to store coal. In the ten years during which they lived in the house, the ghost never walked again. Maybe his walk-by date had expired.

21

Fear of Fear Itself

'Courage is the first of human qualities,' Winston Churchill wrote. 'Because it is the quality which guarantees all others.'

We admire courage and we love the courageous. Every ruler of every nation that has an army or a fire fighting service or a police force ends up pinning medals on individuals from those services who have demonstrated exceptional valour. Former British Prime Minister Gordon Brown sums it up.

'People of courage will always be loved, because they ennoble the human race to which we all belong. We are drawn to them and revere them because, through their actions, they open up the possibility of hope in times of cynicism, dignity in times of degradation, and purpose in times of despair. They give us glimpses of the nobility of which humanity is capable. They raise our sight and challenge us all to be all that we are capable of being. They answer the human hunger for meaning and invest in our human condition a value so great as to assure its pricelessness.'

It was Franklin Delano Roosevelt who coined the phrase. In the depths of the Great Depression, he told his people that they had 'nothing to fear but fear itself.'

The fact, however, is that the fear of fear itself is widely held and can be an onerous burden. It worries individuals that, put to the test, they will show cowardice. They wonder if they would disgrace themselves in situations demanding altruistic courage and selfless bravery. They may even believe that they weren't born with the capacity to become a hero. They think the world is a dangerous place and that – faced with a rapist, a killer or a natural disaster – they may turn into a wimp. Parents have nightmares in which their children are trapped in a fire and they fail to rescue them.

It doesn't help that cowards are the flip side of heroes, particularly in military situations. In the First World War, young, able-bodied men in British cities and town were often presented with white feathers by women who figured that they should have been in uniform, headed for the trenches, and who wanted publicly to register their contempt for them as cowards.

Much worse was the fate that awaited men who crumbled at the front, suffering from what was then called 'shell shock'. More than three hundred British soldiers, some of them Irish, were executed for cowardice or desertion during the conflict. Each and every story that has survived is infinitely sad. Like the young Derry lad, disoriented by repeated shelling, who wandered out into no man's land in complete confusion and wandered back, five days later, looking for his regiment. The following mourning, after being found guilty of desertion, he was executed. A cousin of his who is involved in the Shot at Dawn campaign group, which has helped to bring the British government around to the idea of pardoning the unfortunates who died at the hands of their own colleagues, has pointed out that 'anybody who walks back into his lines again is not planning to desert'. Another man had given nine years of service before it got too much for him and he went absent without leave. One kid of fourteen was so patriotic he added two years to his age in order to get to the front, only to be shot at seventeen – when he was still too young to be officially a member of his regiment.

Every one of them was labelled a coward and executed by the men beside whom they had marched and fought. In the last few years, the British government has issued pardons to many of the men, recognising that the executions – and the damage done to their families by association with a convicted coward – were harshly cruel and in most cases unjustified.

A particularly sad case is that of Private Harry Farr, who volunteered to fight for his country as soon as war broke out. Then he began to get sick with 'nerves' or 'shell shock' and eventually refused to go into the trenches. He was immediately found guilty of 'misbehaving before the enemy in such a manner as to show cowardice' and sentenced to death.

If the twenty-five-year old had actually been a coward, he would assuredly not have done what he did at dawn the following day. He refused a blindfold, saying he would look the firing squad in the eye. Which must have been tough on the lads who had to kill a man of whom their chaplain said, 'a finer soldier never lived'.

But even to tell this story is to follow the theme explored in song and story, whether it takes the form of Kenny Rogers's hit 'The Coward of the County', Johnny Cash's 'A Boy Named Sue' or characters like the Cowardly Lion in *The Wizard of Oz*, all of whom start out as cowards only to prove themselves, under stress, to be the opposite. The frequency of this notion in popular culture does not seem to impact on the fears of those who dread the possibility of being revealed as lacking in courage in a world they see as full of threat.

One of the reasons behind the perception of the world as filled with malign possibilities is television. 'If it bleeds, it leads,' is the rubric for story selection in many TV stations. The human interest story involving death, destruction, fire, explosion, illness or tragic loss is viewed as having more impact than almost any other news report. It's a selection process which results in TV news bulletins majoring on fear-generative items.

'People being killed is definitely a good, objective criteria for whether a story is important,' former *Boston Globe* foreign correspondent Tom Palmer has observed. 'And innocent people being killed is better.'

As a consequence, the more you watch TV news, the more likely you are to believe that setting foot outside your front door exposes you to terror and potential trauma. The older you are, the more housebound you are, the more TV you watch, the more frightened you are likely to be. The more mobile you are, the less you stay glued to tonight's disasters on the box and the more people you encounter, the more confident you are likely to be.

Even if you're pretty confident, in the quotidian, you may suffer the underlying fear of being a coward when required to show courage above and beyond the norm. In fact, when major threat eventuates, most people (with the exception of those suffering the Baskerville Effect (see p. 189) or freezing in position (see pages 92-3) come through amazingly well.

Here, again, is where television falsifies reality. In the case of a terrorist attack or a natural disaster like an earthquake, most people manage pretty well and some show exceptional, commonsensical courage. The problem is that the cameras and reporters are often not on site directly after the disaster. NGOs often find that local people spontaneously form bucket brigades to bail water, or take other group action in an orderly and courageous way, but that this is often obscured by the emphasis of mass media on the fire fighters and the rescue teams, with whom they have often travelled into the disaster area. So much so that one study has found that British children, shown pictures of African families looking happy and prosperous, immediately assume 'that's because we have helped them'. The assumption, logically made by the children, is that Africans facing drought or other disaster cannot and do not help themselves.

While fire fighters, development and emergency organis-ations do heroic work, as do peace-keeping forces from the UN or doctors from Médecins Sans Frontières, their presence at the forefront of disasters tends to create the perception that, until they arrived, everybody was sitting around doing nothing and being generally helpless. Since it's easier for media to interview English-speaking commentators from NGO's than to go searching around asking the equivalent of the British reporter's apocryphal question in a war zone: 'Anybody here been raped or speak English?' this, again, contributes to a public view of those commentators as the officer class manageing and helping the largely passive disaster victims. In fact, however, 'ordinary' people who never thought of themselves as heroes and may never again show heroic tendencies, come through in every crisis, demonstrating practical, useful courage and ensuring that they and others survive.

'Survivors aren't fearless,' Laurence Gonzalez says in his study of the subject, *Deep Survival*. 'They use fear: they turn it into anger and focus.'

Not only are survivors and heroes not without fear, but, in addition, they are often the kind of people others regard as least likely to be heroic in a difficult situation. Take Raoul Wallenberg, the man coming from an uninvolved country during the Second World War who saved countless lives.

'Wallenberg – whose story fascinated me as soon as I came across it as a boy growing up in Scotland in the 1950s – was the most unlikely of war heroes,' says former British Prime Minister, Gordon Brown. 'He was a mild-mannered civilian from a privileged background in a neutral country. The lives of his friends and family were barely affected by the mass killings of the war. His homeland was not being desecrated. And he had no previous history as a man of courage. Indeed at just thirty-one years old he would have more likely been called a playboy than a hero of the resistance and subverter of the Holocaust.'

In his twenties, he got – mainly through the intervention of rich relatives – a job in a bank and found himself staying in a boarding house along with some young Jews who had got out of Hitler's Germany. They told him of persecution, of families being ripped asunder, of lives lost. But they managed to do it in a way that impressed the young banker. They were not passive victims.

'Poor people, they evidently have to adjust to being in a minority wherever they go,' he wrote. 'They have boundless enthusiasm and idealism.'

Nobody would have guessed that Wallenberg's affection

for a small number of Jews of his own age would one day be transformed into a one-man crusade, not least because, when war broke out, he showed no courage at all. He carried a revolver around with him, not because he actually planned to use it, but as a way of boosting his not-terribly-evident courage.

'Raoul was not a brave man by nature,' a friend of his later said, 'During the air raids he was always the first to seek shelter and he was sometimes affected when the bombs fell too close.'

And yet. And yet. This shivering wimp, when he found himself working for Sweden's diplomatic service in Budapest in 1944, decided he had to save some of the Jews there who had not already been rounded up by Adolf Eichmann, Hitler's man on the spot. (Or perhaps, given Eichmann's personality and approach, it would be better to call him Hitler's automaton on the spot.) Wallenberg began to issue protective Swedish passports.

'We have to rid the Jews of the feeling they have been forgotten,' he insisted to anyone who would listen to him.

It was as if, somewhere along the line, someone had injected courage into him. He took his great unwieldy typewriter in the car with him wherever he went, so that he could type out a passport for any Jew he encountered along the road. He waded into processions of Jews being herded towards trains (and towards extermination) by SS men, jamming folded Swedish *Schutzpasses* into their hands and hissing at them to get out of the procession and claim Swedish citizenship. He employed Jews at the Swedish legation, making up food parcels for distribution in the ghettoes. He even met Eichmann face to face in the final days of the war, as the Red Army came within miles of Budapest and it was clear to the Nazi that all was lost, except his Nazi faith and fanaticism, which led him to promise Wallenberg that he would continue shipping Jews out of the city no matter what eventually happened to him

'I warn you, therefore, Herr Legationssekretar,' he told Wallenberg, 'that I will do my best to stop you, and your Swedish diplomatic passport will not help you if I find it necessary to have you removed. Accidents do happen, even to a neutral diplomat.'

Indeed they do, and indeed one did, a few days after their meeting, when Wallenberg's unoccupied car was crushed by a heavy military truck.

Yet he kept going, reporting with factual understatement to his bosses, at the end of the year, that it had been 'possible to rescue some two thousand persons from deportation through intervention for some reason or another.'

The interventions required the man who had once been seen to cower when bombs fell uncomfortably close to where he was sheltering to demonstrate a courage he had never claimed to have.

'He stood out there in the street,' a survivor wrote, 'probably feeling the loneliest man in the world, trying to pretend there was something behind him. They could have shot him there and then in the street and nobody would have known about it. Instead, they relented. He must have had incredible charisma, some great personal authority, because there was absolutely nothing behind him, nothing to back him up.'

As a result of one intervention after another by Wallenberg, when the Soviets entered Budapest they found almost 125,000 Jews alive in various refuges within the city. But in the chaos, the man himself disappeared and was never found, although his family devoted decades to the search. At thirty-three, his life may have ended in a Soviet Gulag or an unmarked grave. Nobody knows. All we know is that a man described by his sister as 'definitely not the square-jawed hero type, more of an anti-hero,' a man who had been unable to conceal his terror at the noise and percussion of falling bombs, somehow found within himself the courage to become, as one of the Jews he saved put it, 'More of a hero than the heroes of old. He did good for the sake of doing good. He never made any demands and he never expected any thanks.'

He is, however, at least remembered, post factum, as a hero. His Japanese counterpart, Chiune Sugihara, who survived the war, encountered exclusion and contempt in post-war Japan and died embittered and largely forgotten. Sugihara was the Japanese Consul-General in Lithuania, who, in 1940, sent a telegram to his government.

'Hundreds of Jewish people have come to the Consulate here in Kaunas seeking transit visas. They are suffering extremely. As a fellow human being, I cannot refuse their requests. Please permit me to issue visas to them.'

The answer was speedy. It was also negative. Yet the diplomat, despite being hardened in the crucible of a hierarchical culture which placed huge value on obedience to orders from a superior, started to write visas by hand. In the process, he saved the lives of at least 3500 Jews, but did so in the certain knowledge that, were he to survive what his homeland must construe as treachery, it would be as a humiliated pariah in Japan. When he died, just twenty-five years ago, he was an impoverished outcast. He was a forgotten hero. A hero because he had faced the abyss and made the sacrificial choice, knowing the dire consequences for himself.

Self-sacrifice in the interests of others, or to vindicate an ideal, is often seen as an essentially male endeavour, partly because so many historical figures who sacrificed their chances for survival for a cause or colleague were from a military background. In this context, it's worth pointing out that Anne Devlin, an outstanding example of Irish heroism, was neither male nor military. Hired by Robert Emmet as his housekeeper to make his home look like an ordinary suburban establishment, rather than the hotbed of subversion it was, Anne was arrested and tortured for information after his disorganised uprising. Despite being repeatedly hanged to the point of unconsciousness, then revived for another round, and despite offers of substantial bribes, she wouldn't talk, even when Emmet told her that betraying him could do him no harm, since he would be executed anyway.

Fear of Failure: Kakorrhaphiophobia

It's the done thing, these days, to be ambitious. To have goals. To have a five-year plan. Anybody who doesn't have one or all of these may be accused of being afraid of failure. But American author, Daniel H. Pink, looking at a study of students graduating from the University of Rochester, suggests we be careful what we strive for. The students were interviewed a year and a half after they left university and joined the workforce.

The people who wanted to do something useful with their lives were a hell of a lot happier than those who had aimed to reach a certain salary level.

'Those who said they were attaining their goals: accumulating wealth, winning acclaim: reported levels of satisfaction, self-esteem, and positive affect no higher than when they were students. In other words, they'd reached their goals, but it didn't make them any happier. What's more, graduates with profit goals showed increases in anxiety, depression, and other negative indicators: again, even though they were attaining their goals.'

Fear of failure is a good spur. Fear of failure to achieve status and money is a mistake. They genuinely don't deliver happiness.

Another situational hero, who rose to the unprecedented demands of her times with a courage she didn't know she had, emerged on 1 December, 1955, in segregated Montgomery, Alabama. That was when Rosa Parks, an African-American seamstress, was ordered by bus driver James Blake to cede her seat on the bus to a white passengers. She baulked, not out of a desire to be a hero, but because she was simply too tired to get up and go to what was then seen as her proper place. At the end of a long day's work, it was one demand too far. Rosa Parks was a civil rights activist, but she took her action that night as a private individual demeaned once too often. It wasn't the first refusal by an African-American to yield to a white person but it was the one that sparked most reaction and was seen as having had pivotal influence. It had required enormous courage, too. A frail child and small adult, Parks wasn't a fighting woman. Nor – after years of civil rights work in the South – could she have been in any doubt about the probable consequences of her high-profile refusal. Within days, she was fired from her job, and her life, thereafter, was never easy. But by gathering her crumbs of courage around her on that day in Montgomery, she changed history.

Today's wimp can become tomorrow's hero. The common thread seems to be the sense that courage is called for, not for oneself, but for others. Given that condition, individuals who have never demonstrated conspicuous courage and who may even have believed themselves incapable of bravery, can astonish themselves by what they do.

The Baskerville Effect

This is named after Sir Charles Baskerville, a character in Arthur Conan Doyle's *The Hound of the Baskervilles*, who dies of a heart attack induced by the fearsome dog of the title. David Phelps and colleagues at the University of California discovered that deaths among Chinese and Japanese were markedly higher on one day of the month – because, apparently, of the association of the number of that day with death in Chinese, Japanese and Korean cultures. The theory is that deaths rise because of the stress associated with the superstition. A parallel suggests that people in the west tend to somehow hold off dying in order to celebrate a particularly auspicious anniversary or occasion, and succumb directly thereafter.

Bibliography

Armstrong, Karen. *A Short History of Myth*. Edinburgh: Canongate, 2005.

Bostridge. Mark. *Florence Nightingale*. New York: Farrar, Straus & Giroux, 2008.

Brooks, David. *On Paradise Drive*. New York: Simon & Schuster, 2004.

Brown, Gordon. *Courage: Portraits of Bravery in the Service of Great Causes*. New York: Weinstein Books, 2008.

Clare, Anthony. *In the Psychiatrist's Chair*. London: William Heinemann, 1992.

de Botton, Alain. *The Art of Travel*. London: Penguin, 2002.

Dobbs, Lou. *War on the Middle Class*. New York: Viking, 2006.

Ekirch, Roger. *At Day's Close*. New York: William Norton, 2005.

Franklin, Jonathan. *33 Men*. New York: Putnam, 2011.

Friend, David. *Watching The World Change: The Stories behind the Images of 9/11*. New York: Farrar, Straus & Giroux, 2004.

Gaines, Steven. *Heroes and Villains: The True Story of the Beach Boys*. New York: New American Library, 1986.

Gawande, Atul. *Better: A Surgeon's Notes on Performance*. Los Angeles: Metropolitan Books, 2007.

Gill, Gillian. *Nightingales*. New York: Random House, 2004.

Gladwell, Malcolm. *Blink*. New York: Little, Brown and Co., 2005.

Kastenbaum, Robert and Ruth Aisenberg. *The Psychology of Death*. London: Duckworth, 1974.

McDermott, Eoghan. *The Career Doctor*. Dublin: Currach Press, 2009.

MacPherson, Malcolm (ed.). *The Black Box: Cockpit Voice Recorder Accounts of In-flight Accidents*. London: HarperCollins, 1998.

Maister, David H., Charles H. Green and Robert M. Galford. *The Trusted Advisor*. New York: Free Press, 2000.

Phillips, Gerald M. *Help for Shy People*. New York: Barnes & Noble, 1981.

Pink, Daniel H. *Drive*. New York: Riverhead Press, 2009.

Prone, Terry and Kieran Lyons. *This Business of Writing: The Irish Guide to Writing and Editing*. Dublin: The Institute of Chartered Accountants in Ireland, 2006.

Prone, Terry. *Talk the Talk*. Dublin: Currach Press 2007.

Reilly, Benjamin. *Tropical Surge*. Sarasota, Florida: Pineapple Press, 2005.

Roach, Mary. *Stiff: The Curious Lives of Human Cadavers*. New York: William Norton, 2004.

Roach, Mary. *Spook: Science Tackles the Afterlife*. New York: William Norton, 2005.

Schneier, Franklin, MD, and Paul Waldman. *Being Right Is Not Enough*. New York: Wiley, 2006.

Schneier, Franklin, MD, and Lawrence Welkowitz PhD. *The Hidden Face of Shyness*. New York: Avon 1996.

Schott, Ben. *Schott's Almanac*. London: Bloomsbury, 2009.

Schwartz, Tony. *The Way We're Working Isn't Working*. New York: Free Press, 2010.

Sheehan, George, MD. *Going the Distance*. New York: Villard, 1996.

Sherwood, Ben. *The Survivors Club*. New York: Grand Central, 2010.

Weiner, Eric. *The Geography of Bliss*. New York: Twelve, 2008.

Wilkins, Robert. *Death: A History of Man's Obsessions and Fears*. New York: Barnes & Noble, 1990.

Wilson, Colin and Damon Wilson, *The Mammoth Book of Illustrated Crime*. New York: Carroll & Graf, 2002.

Wilson, Timothy D. *Strangers to Ourselves*. Harvard: Belknap Press 2002.

Worsley, Lucy. *If Walls Could Talk: An Intimate History of the Home*. London: Faber and Faber 2011.